MACRO COOKBOOK FOR BEGINNERS

HOW TO GET LEAN AND STAY FIT WITH MACRO DIET RECIPES. INCLUDES A 30-DAY MEAL PLAN

D1522958

Table of Contents

Introduction

Macro dieting has become more popular as a means of weight loss. This is attributed to the low-carb, high-protein dieting trend, which in turn brings more attention to the idea of eating carbs and proteins while minimizing fat intake. A macro diet is one that uses these food groups to make up a day's worth of eating (in addition to vegetables). Though the term "macro" implies that it focuses on protein as a nutrient, it actually also includes carbohydrates and fat. The idea is that these nutrients should be eaten and consumed in proportions that will help people lose weight, increase energy, and improve body composition.

A macro diet is an eating plan wherein a person's daily intake of calories is broken down into specific macronutrients (proteins, carbohydrates, and fats). This type of dieting is considered to be a high-protein diet because it is usually comprised of high amounts of protein. This makes up for the fact that it is low in fat, which is the last nutrient considered to be essential (you need fat, but not so much that you exceed your daily caloric intake).

Why People Implement Macros

In order to understand why people choose to implement macros as a means to lose weight or increase muscle mass, you first need to understand what macros are and how they can help people. Basically, macronutrients are the three types of nutrients that can be found in food. The first two macros are carbohydrates and protein. Carbohydrates and sugar are used by the body to convert into glucose, which is burned for energy. Protein is used to build muscle mass through a process called anabolism. The third macro is fat, which helps you feel full when you eat something fatty because it takes longer than carbohydrates or protein to digest.

Using a Macro Diet to Lose Weight

Many people choose to eat a macro diet because they want to lose weight, and they believe that it will help them achieve this goal. If you are someone who desires to lose weight, then you should know that this is an effective strategy for losing a considerable amount of body fat. The reason for this is because the bulk of your daily caloric intake should be from protein. This is because the body burns more calories when the protein you are consuming is used to build up muscle mass.

However, it is important that you don't take in too much protein. The recommended weight loss percentage shown on most diet plans for women is about 10–20% of total calories from protein. Some people may recommend higher percentages, but this too should be done with caution. If you consume too much fat and carbohydrates, then the amount of lean muscle tissue that your body will provide itself will decline. This may result in a smaller amount of muscle being created, which will have an impact on your overall weight loss.

Why People Implement Macros to Increase Muscle Mass

You should know that losing weight can be beneficial for building muscle mass. What many people don't realize is that you can also benefit from gaining weight, which is why macros become important when trying to gain lean muscle mass. Eating macros will help you lose fat while building up lean muscle mass in the process. This is one of the main reasons why you can find many men and women trying to improve their body composition by implementing macronutrients as a means to building muscle mass while losing fat.

Chapter 1. What the Macro Diet is and its benefits

The macro diet is a way of eating that focuses on tracking your daily macronutrient intake. Rather than avoiding certain foods, you use macros as a tool to find balance in your diet.

Three macronutrients make up every bite of food you eat: protein, carbohydrates, and fat. Although it's important to get the majority of your energy from nutrient-dense energy sources, no foods are off-limits on the macro diet as long as you stay within your daily macro targets. For this reason, it is sometimes referred to as the "if it fits your macros" (IIFYM) diet or "flexible eating." In other words, you can have your cake and eat it, too, as long as it fits your macros and the majority of your diet consists of high-fiber carbs, lean protein, and healthy fats.

Our bodies are often compared to cars that need fuel in the form of calories to function. And although this is true to some extent, it fails to take into account the type of fuel you put into your proverbial tank. Yes, you can derive energy from whatever calories you consume, but behind the scenes, serious havoc may be unfolding. This, in turn, can impact your ability to manage your weight.

Why Many Diets Fail

The big reason that so many modern diets fail is that they revolve around the restriction, which, as many of us know, is hard to maintain in the long run. For instance, the low-carb keto diet means swearing off bread and pasta. When we focus on what we can't eat—rather than the foods we can and should fill our plate with—we encourage a cycle of craving, "slipups," and guilt that can promote an unhealthy relationship with eating.

Although it's true that you can shed pounds on crash diets when you expend more calories than you consume, this rapid weight loss often entails the loss of water and muscle, not just body fat. This is not desirable. Losing mass muscle impacts your metabolism because, at rest, muscle burns more calories than fat.

All too often, these factors lead to weight cycling, which is the loss and gain of the same number of pounds before and after dieting. After depriving yourself of certain foods for a period of time, you are likely to feel more tempted than ever to eat them once a diet is finished. And rapid weight loss is often undone as you put back on water weight and have less muscle to help burn fat.

Why the Macro Diet Works

The macro diet is not the new kid on the block. Rather than promising a newfound secret to get fit quickly, it relies on tried-and-true principles of nutrition. We'll look in more detail at the science of the diet soon, but in simple terms, macro eating is so successful because it does away with the idea that you can never eat certain foods because you can have them as long as you are hitting your daily macro targets.

As you'll learn, although no foods are off-limits, it's important to consume nutrient-dense foods most of the time to see results.

The Key Health Benefits of Macro Diets

The macro diet is adaptable to any lifestyle and schedule, and it offers many benefits for both the body and mind.

- **Better Relationship with Food**: The "all foods fit" approach allows you to enjoy your favorite foods without feeling deprived or guilty.
- **Builds Muscle:** Although building muscle requires a combination of strength training and consuming more energy than you burn, adjusting your macro ratios—especially when it comes to protein—will help you build and preserve muscle tissue.
- **Long-Term Health:** Learning how to fuel your body with nutrient-dense meals like the recipes in this book—and eating less-healthy foods in moderation—can help you establish lifelong eating patterns that promote long-term health.
- **Weight Loss:** Macro eating increases the awareness of food quality and quantity and allows better appetite control to support your weight goals. Consuming meals with adequate amounts of protein and healthy fats helps slow down the emptying of food from the stomach into the intestine. Consuming enough high-fiber carbohydrates adds bulk to food to slow down its passage through the body. Together, nutrient-dense sources of all three macronutrients will help you feel fuller.

Chapter 2.   Tips and indications on the amount of calories to be taken

We already know that calories come from macros. By definition, when you are tracking your macros, you will always know exactly how many calories you have consumed in a day. What is important is that the total number of macros you consume correlates with the number of calories you require. You will need a deficit to lose weight and a surplus to gain muscle.

In this sense, it is important to recognize that not all calories are equal. For example, a chocolate bar and a handful of almonds may each have 200 calories, but the chocolate bar is going to be full of simple carbohydrates in the form of added sugar, which can cause your blood sugar level to spike, then quickly leave you feeling flat. What's more, it will lack the fiber, healthy fats, and proteins of almonds that keep you feeling full longer and provide sustained energy release.

Instead of approaching the macro diet as "giving up" calories, shift your mindset to focus on adding foods that will best help meet your carbohydrate, protein, and fat targets.

Have your cake and eat it, too

A good guideline to follow when it comes to how to balance wholesome foods and treats is the 80/20 rule. This means eating natural, wholesome foods like fresh produce most of the time (80%), leaving some room (20%) to enjoy treats or foods like cookies.

Here is a general rule to help maximize that 80% of your diet: divide your plate into three sections with half of the plate vegetables and fruits, a quarter of the plate lean protein, and a quarter of the plate whole grains and a source of healthy fat. With time, you'll be able to identify your macronutrient portions with ease, making this approach more sustainable.

A closer look at macros

The diet industry bombards us with confusing and often conflicting messages around what we should and shouldn't eat. The truth is that no macronutrient is inherently "bad" for you, as long as you are eating enough of the right types. Although the recipes and meal plan in this book contain all the best sorts of macros to nourish your body, the following pages will teach you about the importance of each.

In defense of carbs

In recent decades, the success of the low-carb Atkins diet and more recently the ketogenic diet has made this macronutrient more maligned than any other. The truth of the matter is that eating carbs will not automatically cause you to gain weight; excess consumption of *any* macronutrient will.

Unlike protein and fat, carbs are the body's preferred energy source. They're broken down into sugar molecules (glucose) that cells readily take up and use as fuel. Although some glucose is stored as glycogen in muscles and the liver, excess may be converted into body fat.

Carbs are comprised of three components: fiber, starches, and sugars.

- **Fiber:** abundant in many foods like fruits and vegetables, fiber is unique in that it does not break down during digestion, which means that it has a minimal caloric impact. Fiber helps with:
    - Bowel regulation and gut health
    - Improving blood cholesterol levels that support heart health
    - Controlling blood sugar levels
- **Starches:** Made up of longer chains of sugar molecules, starches are referred to as complex carbs, which take longer to digest. This leads to less of a blood sugar spike, longer-lasting energy, and less hunger.
- **Sugars:** These are made up of one or a few sugar molecules, giving them the name "simple carbohydrates." Some sugars occur naturally (like in fruit) and others are added into foods (like table sugar). According to the 2015–2020 dietary guidelines for Americans and Heart & Stroke Canada, added sugars should be limited to less than 10% of total daily calories. Unlike naturally occurring sugars that are found in foods that contribute other nutrients and fiber, added sugars provide no nutritional value.

The power of protein

There is a good reason protein has celebrity status when it comes to weight loss: it requires more energy to digest than other macronutrients. In other words, it has a greater thermic effect, one of the components that impacts metabolism.

Protein provides energy and is part of every cell in the body. Proteins are made up of multiple building blocks known as amino acids, some of which the body synthesizes on its own (nonessential) and others that need to be obtained from the diet (essential).

Essential amino acids must be consumed daily because they cannot be stored in the body, and limited amounts impact the production of muscle and body tissue proteins. By consuming a diet that includes a variety of protein sources, one can obtain adequate amounts of essential amino acids.

Protein is best known for its role in the growth and repair of body and muscle cells, in particular with exercise. Consuming adequate amounts of protein after a workout provides the body with the amino acids it needs to decrease muscle breakdown and support muscle growth—muscle burns more calories than fat at rest. Other functions of protein include:

- Producing enzymes, hormones, and body chemicals to carry out metabolic reactions

- Transporting nutrients
- Muscle contraction
- Promoting the feeling of fullness

Why do you need fats

Despite what you may have heard, fats are an essential nutrient that your body needs. Although it's true that low-fat diets were once the "it" thing to lose weight, research actually suggests that this information is outdated, and for good reason. Fats are a part of every single cell in your body, making it impossible to live without them. Some of the main functions of fats include:

- Absorbing and transporting fat-soluble vitamins (a, d, e, k)
- Slowing down the emptying of food from the stomach into the intestine, which promotes the feeling of fullness
- Producing hormones
- Regulating cholesterol levels and heart health

It's important to note that not all dietary fats (saturated, trans, polyunsaturated, monounsaturated) are created equally nor are they automatically stored as body fat. In fact, weight gain and an increase in body fat occur when any nutrient is consumed more than the body requires. Since the type of dietary fat impacts the body differently, it's important to choose wisely.

Solid fats (trans and saturated) can raise low-density lipoprotein (LDL), known as "bad" cholesterol, which is linked to a higher risk of cardiovascular disease. On the contrary, unsaturated fats (monounsaturated and polyunsaturated) can help improve the levels of high-density lipoprotein (HDL), known as "good" cholesterol.

The supporting cast: micronutrients

There is one final category of nutrients that we haven't looked at yet: micronutrients. Although they are only needed in small amounts and are not a source of energy, they provide essential vitamins and minerals that allow your body to function at an optimal level.

They also play a huge role in metabolic reactions, including energy metabolism, which involves a series of biochemical reactions that enzymes support. Some of these enzymes require coenzymes or cofactors, of which many are vitamins. For example, thiamine (vitamin B_1) is involved in carbohydrate metabolism. A deficiency in thiamine could not only impact this process but can manifest as neurological disorders.

Chapter 3.   Calculating the Macro ratio

The chemical compounds you consume are known as macros. A nutrition label shows how many grams of each macronutrient (carbohydrates, proteins, and fats) are included in a single serving. Macros have a variety of roles in body optimization. "We cannot exist without all three of these macronutrients, even for a short period of time "They're necessary for everything from growth and development to supporting circulation and supplying enough energy for cognitive functioning."

- Carbohydrates (glucose) are the body's primary energy source. Immediately put to use. Muscles or fat are stored for later use.
- Proteins (amino acids)—aid in the growth and maintenance of lean muscle mass.
- Hormones are regulated by fats (fatty acids).
- All macros provide energy to our bodies.
    - Per gram 5 calories of carbohydrate
    - Per gram 5 calories of protein
    - Per gram 8 calories of fat

Macronutrients and calories are related when it comes to weight gain or decrease. Macro ratios, on the other hand, can affect body composition.

The Most Appropriate Macro Ratio for Your Phenotype

A 21-year-old male football player's physique differs dramatically from that of a sedentary 52-year-old female. Ectomorph, mesomorph, and endomorph are the three body types that everyone has. Depending on their bodily composition, some people are a mix of the two. As a result, applying a "one size fits all" approach to macro ratios would be counterproductive. Based on how your body reacts to different macronutrient percentages, you may need to adjust your macro amounts.

However, everyone must start from the beginning. It's just as important to know where to begin as it is to take the first step. These three macronutrient ratios (depending on your phenotype) will help you save time and money on your fitness quest. The macro ratios given below are recommended as a foundation by Obi Obadike, MS, ISSA Certified Fitness Trainer, and Nutrition Specialist.

What Macro Ratio Is Best for You Based On Your Phenotype (Body Shape)?

Ectomorph is the first body type

- Skinny
- Frame with a narrow width
- Has a hard time gaining weight (muscle or fat)
- A quick metabolism
- Tolerance to carbohydrates is high.

Ectomorphs' Macro Ratio

- Carbohydrates comprise 55% of the total.
- Protein accounts for 25% of the total.
- Λ fat content of 20%

Mesomorph is the second body kind

- Mesomorphs have a muscular and athletic body.
- Shoulders that are wider and a waist that is narrower
- Muscle gain is simple.
- Can put on weight faster than an ectomorph.
- A frame that is symmetrical

Mesomorphs' Macro Ratio

- 40% of the calories come from carbs.
- 30% of the ingredients are proteins.
- A fat content of 30%

Endomorph is the third body type

- Gains weight quickly.
- Muscle gain is simple.
- A bigger frame
- Has a hard time shedding weight
- Tolerance to carbohydrates is low

Endomorphs' Macro Ratio

- 25% of calories come from carbs.
- Proteins provide about 35% of the total
- 40% of calories come from fat.

Don't eat like Sam if your body type is comparable to Pete's. That's a tragedy waiting to happen.

Tools that will guide You in Setting Up Your Macro Numbers

How to Work Out Your Macro Numbers

It is perfectly possible to compute the number of glucose, protein, and fat grams you require on a daily basis by hand. This gives you great control and freedom over the numbers you want to enter.

However, for many people, this is time-consuming and tedious. There are varieties of tools available online to help you calculate your macro figures. Many of these sites also evaluate your objectives (fat reduction, maintenance, or muscle mass gain). Here are a few examples:

If It Fits Your Macros—If you've never computed your macros before, this calculator is the most complete.

Katy Hearn Fit—You can modify your nutrition plan with this one. You have the option of allocating how many grams of protein and fat per pound of body weight.

Tracking Calories &Tracking Macros

Because they are striving to achieve certain fitness or performance goals, some people, particularly athletes, track their macronutrient intake rather than their calorie intake. A person's macro intake can also help them manage a medical condition. People with type 2 diabetes, for example, frequently count carbs to regulate and limit their intake.

There are advantages and disadvantages to counting calories and macros; the optimal way for you will be determined by your objectives.

What's the Point of Calorie Counting?

If your objective is to lose weight, your program's success or failure will be determined by your overall calorie consumption. You won't lose weight unless you regularly establish a significant calorie deficit. You'll probably need to consume a modified version of your weight loss calorie goal to maintain your weight.

People who are trying to lose weight or keep it off frequently keep track of their calories. Calorie counting is straightforward and takes little time or effort. Most foods and beverages have calorie numbers printed right on the Nutrition Facts label. If it isn't there, there are nutrition databases online or in smartphone apps that provide correct numbers.

Why Should Macronutrients Be Monitored?

Despite the fact that tracking calories is simple (requiring just one number), some people prefer to track macros instead. Macronutrient tracking is more difficult since you must set goals for three intake numbers rather than just one. These figures can be useful for persons who are aiming to achieve fitness objectives or lose weight.

Should You Monitor Your Macros?

People who are attempting to lose weight, for example, may find that getting more of their daily calories from protein makes it easier to meet their calorie goal. Protein, when included in every meal, may help you eat less since it delivers more satiety than carbohydrates.

People with heart disease or a similar condition should keep track of their fat consumption, particularly saturated fat, to lower their risk of a cardiac attack.

People who are aiming to achieve fitness objectives frequently keep track of their macronutrients. Endurance athletes, for example, may aim for a specific carb intake to ensure that they are appropriately fed for a race. Strength-trained athletes may want to limit their protein intake in order to achieve their performance goals.

Chapter 4. Breakfast

1. Almond with Yogurt Parfait

Preparation time: 10 minutes
Cooking time: 3 minutes
Servings: 6
Ingredients:

- 2½ cups rolled oats
- ¾ cup slivered almonds
- 6 tbsp. puffed rice cereal
- 6 tbsp. raisins
- 4½ tbsp. hemp hearts
- 4½ tbsp. pepitas
- ¾ tsp. ground cinnamon
- 6 cups non-fat plain Greek yogurt
- 4½ cups fresh raspberries

Directions:

1. Cook the oats in a nonstick skillet over medium heat, stirring continuously, until lightly brown, 2 to 3 minutes. Transfer the browned oats to a large bowl.
2. Add the almonds, rice cereal, raisins, hemp hearts, pepitas, and cinnamon to the oats and mix well. Divide the mixture into 6 servings.
3. To assemble the parfaits: Layer each of 6 glasses with ½ cup of Greek yogurt, ¼ cup of raspberries, a ¼ serving of the oat mixture, ½ cup of Greek yogurt, ¼ cup of raspberries, and the remaining ¼ serving of the oat mixture. Serve immediately.

Nutrition:
Calories: 240 | Fat: 14 g | Protein: 35 g | Sodium: 96 mg | Fiber: 9 g | Carbohydrates: 52 g | Sugar: 3 g

2. Blueberry Fat Bombs

Preparation time: 10 minutes
Cooking time: 0 minutes
Servings: 12
Ingredients:

- 1/2 cup blueberries, mashed
- 1/2 cup coconut oil, at room temperature
- 1/2 cup cream cheese, at room temperature
- A pinch nutmeg
- 6 drops liquid stevia

Directions:

1. Line the 12-cup muffin tin with 12 paper liners.
2. Put all the ingredients and process until it has a thick and mousse-like consistency.
3. Pour the mixture into the 12 cups of the muffin tin. Put the muffin tin into the refrigerator to chill for 1 to 3 hours.

Nutrition:
Calories: 120 | Fat: 12.5 g | Fiber: 1.4 g | Carbohydrates: 2.1 g | Protein: 3.1 g

3. Cheesy Zucchini Triangles with Garlic Mayo Dip

Preparation time: 20 minutes
Cooking time: 30 minutes
Servings: 4
Ingredients:
Garlic Mayo Dip:

- 1 cup crème Fraiche
- 1/3 cup mayonnaise
- 1/4 tsp. sugar-free maple syrup
- 1 garlic clove, pressed
- 1/2 tsp. vinegar
- Salt and black pepper to taste

Cheesy Zucchini Triangles:

- 2 large zucchinis, grated
- 1 egg
- 1/4 cup almond flour
- 1/4 tsp. paprika powder
- 3/4 tsp. dried mixed herbs
- 1/4 tsp. swerve sugar
- 1/2 cup grated mozzarella cheese

Directions:

1. Start by making the dip; in a medium bowl, mix the crème Fraiche, mayonnaise, maple syrup, garlic, vinegar, salt, and black pepper.
2. Cover the bowl with a plastic wrap and refrigerate while you make the zucchinis.
3. Let the oven preheat at 400°F. And line a baking tray with greaseproof paper. Set aside.
4. Put the zucchinis in a cheesecloth and press out as much liquid as possible.
5. Pour the zucchinis into a bowl.
6. Add the egg, almond flour, paprika, dried mixed herbs, and swerve sugar.
7. Mix well and spread the mixture on the baking tray into a round pizza-like piece with 1-inch thickness.
8. Let it bake for 25 minutes.
9. Reduce the oven's heat to 350°F/175°C, take out the tray, and sprinkle the zucchini with the mozzarella cheese.
10. Let it melt in the oven.
11. Remove afterward, set aside to cool for 5 minutes, and then slice the snacks into triangles.
12. Serve immediately with the garlic mayo dip.

Nutrition:
Calories: 286 | Fat: 11.4 g | Fiber: 8.4 g | Carbohydrates: 4.3 g | Protein: 10.1 g

4. Herbed Cheese Chips

Preparation time: 15 minutes
Cooking time: 15 minutes
Servings: 8
Ingredients:

- 3 tbsp. coconut flour
- 1/2 cup strong cheddar cheese, grated and divided
- 1/4 cup Parmesan cheese, grated
- 2 tbsp. butter, melted
- 1 organic egg
- 1 tsp. fresh thyme leaves, minced

Directions:

1. Preheat the oven to 350°F. Line a large baking sheet with parchment paper.
2. In a bowl, place the coconut flour, 1/4 cup of grated cheddar, Parmesan, butter, and the egg, and mix until well combined.
3. Make eight equal-sized balls from the mixture.
4. Arrange the balls onto a prepared baking sheet in a single layer about 2-inch apart.
5. Form into flat discs.
6. Sprinkle each disc with the remaining cheddar, followed by thyme.
7. Bake for around 15 minutes.

Nutrition:
Calories: 101 | Fat: 6.5 g | Fiber: 1.4 g | Carbohydrates: 1.2 g | Protein: 3.1 g

5. Cauliflower Poppers

Preparation time: 20 minutes
Cooking time: 30 minutes
Servings: 4
Ingredients:

- 4 cups cauliflower florets
- 2 tsp. olive oil
- 1/4 tsp. chili powder
- Pepper and salt

Directions:

1. Preheat the oven to 450°F. Grease a roasting pan.
2. In a bowl, add all ingredients and toss to coat well.
3. Transfer the cauliflower mixture into a prepared roasting pan and spread in an even layer.
4. Roast for about 25–30 minutes.
5. Serve warm.

Nutrition:
Calories: 102 | Fat: 8.5 g | Fiber: 4.7 g | Carbohydrates: 2.1 g | Protein: 4.2 g

6. Crispy Parmesan Chips

Preparation time: 10 minutes
Cooking time: 5 minutes
Servings: 8
Ingredients:

- 1 tsp. butter
- 8 ounces full-fat Parmesan cheese, shredded or freshly grated

Directions:

1. Preheat the oven to 400°F.
2. The Parmesan cheese must be spooned onto the baking sheet in mounds, spread evenly apart.
3. Spread out the mounds with the back of a spoon until they are flat.
4. Bake the crackers until the edges are browned, and the centers are still pale, about 5 minutes.

Nutrition:
Calories: 101 | Fat: 9.4 g | Fiber: 3.1 g | Carbohydrates: 2.5 g | Protein: 1.2 g

7. Tex-Mex Queso Dip

Preparation time: 5 minutes
Cooking time: 10 minutes
Servings: 6
Ingredients:

- 1/2 cup coconut milk
- 1/2 jalapeño pepper, seeded and diced
- 1 tsp. minced garlic
- 1/2 tsp. onion powder
- 1-ounce goat cheese
- 6 ounces sharp Cheddar cheese, shredded
- 1/4 tsp. cayenne pepper

Directions:

1. Preheat a pot then add the coconut milk, jalapeño, garlic, and onion powder.
2. Simmer then whisk in the goat cheese until smooth.
3. Add the Cheddar cheese and cayenne and whisk until the dip is thick, 30 seconds to 1 minute.

Nutrition:
Calories: 149 | Fat: 12.1 g | Fiber: 3.1 g | Carbohydrates: 5.1 g | Protein: 4.2 g

8. Sweet Onion Dip

Preparation time: 15 minutes
Cooking time: 25–30 minutes
Servings: 4
Ingredients:
- 3 cup sweet onion chopped
- tsp. pepper sauce
- cups Swiss cheese shredded
- Ground black pepper
- cups mayonnaise
- 1/4 cup horseradish

Directions:
1. Take a bowl, add sweet onion, horseradish, pepper sauce, mayonnaise, and Swiss cheese, mix them well and transfer them to the pie plate.
2. Preheat oven to 375°F.
3. Now put the plate into the oven and bake for 25 to 30 minutes until edges turn golden brown.
4. Sprinkle pepper to taste and serve with crackers.

Nutrition:
Calories: 278 | Fat: 11.4 g | Fiber: 4.1 g | Carbohydrates: 2.9 g | Protein: 6.9 g

9. Keto Trail Mix

Preparation time: 5 minutes
Cooking time: 0 minutes
Servings: 3
Ingredients:
- 1/2 cup salted pumpkin seeds
- 1/2 cup slivered almonds
- 3/4 cup roasted pecan halves
- 3/4 cup unsweetened cranberries
- 1 cup toasted coconut flakes

Directions:
1. In a skillet, place almonds and pecans. Heat for 2–3 minutes and let cool.
2. Once cooled, in a large resealable plastic bag, combine all ingredients.
3. Seal and shake vigorously to mix.
4. Evenly divide into suggested servings and store in airtight meal prep containers.

Nutrition:
Calories: 98 | Fat: 1.2 g | Fiber: 4.1 g | Carbohydrates: 1.1 g | Protein: 3.2 g

10. Cold Cuts and Cheese Pinwheels

Preparation time: 20 minutes
Cooking time: 0 minutes
Servings: 2
Ingredients:

- 8 ounces cream cheese, at room temperature
- 1/4-pound salami, thinly sliced
- 2 tbsp. sliced pepperoncini

Directions:

1. Layout a sheet of plastic wrap on a large cutting board or counter.
2. Place the cream cheese in the center of the plastic wrap, and then add another layer of plastic wrap on top.
3. Using a rolling pin, roll the cream cheese until it is even and about 1/4 inch thick.
4. Try to make a shape that somewhat resembles a rectangle.
5. Pull off the top layer of plastic wrap.
6. Place the salami slices so they overlap to cover the cream-cheese layer completely.
7. Place a new piece of plastic wrap on top of the salami layer to flip over your cream cheese–salami rectangle.

Flip the layer, so the cream cheese side is up.

8. Remove the plastic wrap and add the sliced pepperoncini in a layer on top.
9. Roll the layered ingredients into a tight log, pressing the meat and cream cheese together. (You want it as tight as possible.)
10. Then wrap the roll with plastic wrap and refrigerate for at least 6 hours so it will set.
11. Slice and serve.

Nutrition:
Calories: 141 | Fat: 4.9 g | Fiber: 2.1 g | Carbohydrates: 0.3 g | Protein: 8.5 g

11. Zucchini Balls with Capers and Bacon

Preparation time: 3 hrs.
Cooking time: 20 minutes
Servings: 10
Ingredients:

- 2 zucchinis, shredded
- 2 bacon slices, chopped
- 1/2 cup cream cheese, at room temperature
- 1 cup fontina cheese
- 1/4 cup capers
- 1 garlic clove, crushed
- 1/2 cup grated Parmesan cheese
- 1/2 tsp. poppy seeds
- 1/4 tsp. dried dill weed

- 1/2 tsp. onion powder
- Salt and black pepper, to taste
- 1 cup crushed pork rinds

Directions:

1. Preheat oven to 360°F.
2. Thoroughly mix zucchinis, capers, 1/2 of Parmesan cheese, garlic, cream cheese, bacon, and fontina cheese until well combined.
3. Shape the mixture into balls.
4. Refrigerate for 3 hours.
5. In a mixing bowl, mix the remaining Parmesan cheese, crushed pork rinds, dill, black pepper, onion powder, poppy seeds, and salt.
6. Roll cheese ball in Parmesan mixture to coat.
7. Arrange in a greased baking dish in a single layer and bake in the oven for 15–20 minutes, shaking once.

Nutrition:
Calories: 227 | Fat: 12.5 g | Fiber: 9.4 g | Carbohydrates: 4.3 g | Protein: 14.5 g

12. Strawberry Fat Bombs

Preparation time: 30 minutes
Cooking time: 0 minutes
Servings: 6

Ingredients:

- 100 g strawberries
- 100 g cream cheese
- 50 g butter
- 2 tbsp. erythritol powder
- 1/2 tsp. vanilla extract

Directions:

1. Put the cream cheese and butter (cut into small pieces) in a mixing bowl.
2. Let rest for 30 to 60 minutes at room temperature.
3. In the meantime, wash the strawberries and remove the green parts.
4. Pour into a bowl and process into a puree with a serving of oil or a mixer.
5. Add erythritol powder and vanilla extract and mix well.
6. Mix the strawberries with the other ingredients and make sure that they have reached room temperature.
7. Put the cream cheese and butter into a container.
8. Mix with a hand mixer or a food processor to a homogeneous mass.
9. Pour the mixture into small silicone muffin molds. Freeze.

Nutrition:
Calories: 95 | Fat: 9.1 g | Fiber: 4.1 g | Carbohydrates: 0.9 g | Protein: 2.1 g

13.   Cinnamon Applesauce Oatmeal

Preparation time: 10 minutes
Cooking time: 6 minutes
Servings: 4
Ingredients:

- 6 large egg whites
- ½ cup oatmeal
- 1 tbsp. unsweetened applesauce
- 1 tsp. cinnamon
- 1 packet stevia
- ¼ tsp. baking soda
- 1 tsp. olive oil
- 1 medium apple, diced

Directions:

1. Heat a medium nonstick pan over medium heat for 5 minutes.
2. Combine all ingredients except oil and apple in a blender, blending until mixed well.
3. Lightly oil the pan, coating all surfaces.
4. Slowly pour ¼ of batter into the pan.
5. When the mixture starts to bubble, top with ¼ of apples and flip.
6. Cook 1 more minute, then serve immediately.

Nutrition:
Calories: 386 | Fat: 8 g | Protein: 27 g | Sodium: 646 mg | Fiber: 8 g | Carbohydrates: 55 g | Sugar: 20 g

14.   Egg and Chocolate French Toast

Preparation time: 10 minutes
Cooking time: 3 minutes
Servings: 1
Ingredients:

- Cooking spray
- 3 large egg whites
- ½ scoop chocolate protein powder
- 2 slices whole-grain bread
- 1 packet stevia
- 1 tsp. cinnamon
- ½ cup sugar-free maple syrup

Directions:

1. Heat a medium skillet over medium-high heat and coat lightly with cooking spray.
2. Whisk together egg whites and protein in a large bowl.
3. Dip bread into egg and protein mixture, coating both sides.
4. Add slices to skillet, cooking 2 to 3 minutes per side or until golden brown.
5. Remove from skillet; top with stevia, cinnamon, and syrup. Serve immediately.

Nutrition:
Calories: 295 | Fat: 2 g | Protein: 29 g | Sodium: 689 mg | Fiber: 3 g | Carbohydrates: 46 g | Sugar: 7 g

15. Egg and Applesauce Banana Muffins

Preparation time: 15 minutes
Cooking time: 30 minutes
Servings: 12
Ingredients:

- 1¼ cups whole-wheat flour
- ¾ tsp. baking soda
- ½ tsp. salt
- 2 tbsp. unsalted butter, softened
- ¼ cup brown sugar (or stevia alternative)
- 2 large egg whites
- 3 ripe medium bananas
- ¼ cup pure maple syrup
- 2 tbsp. unsweetened applesauce
- ½ tsp. vanilla extract
- $^1/_3$ cup crushed pecans

Directions:

1. Preheat oven to 325°F (163°C).
2. Line a 12-cup muffin tin with baking liners.
3. Combine flour, baking soda, and salt in a large bowl and mix well.
4. In a separate large bowl, mix butter and brown sugar until smooth.
5. Add egg whites, bananas, maple syrup, applesauce, and vanilla and mix by hand or with an electric mixer until well blended.
6. Gently stir in flour mixture until combined and then evenly divide into lined muffin cups.
7. Sprinkle muffin tops with pecans and bake 30 to 35 minutes, until a toothpick inserted into the center comes out clean.

Nutrition:
Calories: 143 | Fat: 5 g | Protein: 3 g | Sodium: 191 mg | Fiber: 2.5 g | Carbohydrates: 25 g | Sugar: 7 g

16. Vanilla Whipped Protein Bowl

Preparation time: 5 minutes
Cooking time: 0 minute
Servings: 1
Ingredients:

- ½ cup fat-free Greek yogurt
- 1 scoop vanilla whey protein
- ¼ cup water
- 1 cup frozen mixed berries
- ½ cup fat-free whipped cream

Direction:

1. Combine yogurt, protein, and water in a small bowl, whisking until blended.
2. Let the bowl sit in the freezer for 5 minutes to thicken.
3. Remove from freezer, top with berries and whipped cream, and serve.

Nutrition:
Calories: 333 | Fat: 8 g | Protein: 38 g | Sodium: 86 mg | Fiber: 3.5 g | Carbohydrates: 30 g | Sugar: 22 g

17. Egg and Tortilla Spinach Wrap

Preparation time: 10 minutes
Cooking time: 5 minutes
Servings: 1
Ingredients:

- Cooking spray
- 3 large egg whites
- 1 cup chopped baby spinach
- ¼ cup feta cheese
- 2 tbsp. sun-dried tomatoes, chopped
- 1 medium whole-wheat tortilla

Directions:

1. Heat a medium skillet over medium heat and coat lightly with cooking spray.
2. Scramble egg whites and spinach until fully cooked.
3. Add feta cheese and mix well.
4. Spread the tomatoes in the tortilla, add egg mixture, roll, and serve.

Nutrition:
Calories: 175 | Fat: 8.5 g | Protein: 18 g | Sodium: 549 mg | Fiber: 1.5 g | Carbohydrates: 7 g | Sugar: 5 g

18.   Banana Shake with Peanut Butter

Preparation time: 10 minutes
Cooking time: 0 minute
Servings: 4
Ingredients:

- 4 small bananas
- 2 cups 1% milk
- 1¼ cups rolled oats
- 1 cup non-fat plain Greek yogurt
- 4 tbsp. creamy 100% all-natural peanut butter
- 1 ounce (28 g) dark chocolate (optional)

Directions:

1. Combine the bananas, milk, oats, Greek yogurt, peanut butter, and chocolate (if using) into a blender and puree until smooth.
2. Pour into 4 glasses and serve.
3. Refrigerate any leftovers in a mason jar for up to 24 hours. Shake well before serving.

Nutrition:
Calories: 449| Fat: 15 g; Protein| 22 g; Sodium 80 mg |Fiber: 8 g Carbohydrates: 61 g| Sugar: 53 g

19.   Spinach with Milk Banana Smoothie

Preparation time: 10 minutes
Cooking time: 0 minute
Servings: 2
Ingredients:

- 3 cups fresh baby spinach
- 1 large banana
- 1 cup skim milk
- 1 cup non-fat plain Greek yogurt
- ½ cup fresh blueberries
- $^1/_3$ cup rolled oats
- ⅛ cup 100% all-natural

Directions:

1. Combine the spinach, banana, milk, yogurt, blueberries, oats, almond butter, and hemp hearts in a blender and puree until smooth.
2. Pour into 2 glasses and serve.

Nutrition:
Calories: 383 | Fat: 11 g | Total Carbohydrates: 49 g | Net Carbs: 42 g | Fiber: 7 g | Protein: 26 g | Sodium: 135 mg

20. Raspberry Cheer Overnight Oats

Preparation time: 5 minutes
Cooking time: 0 minute
Servings: 6
Ingredients:

- 3 cups rolled oats
- 6 tbsp. chia seeds
- 4½ cups fresh raspberries
- 6 tbsp. creamy 100% all-natural peanut butter

Directions:

1. Combine 1 cup of Greek yogurt, ½ cup rolled oats, and 1 tbsp. of chia seeds in each of 6 mason jars and mix well.
2. Cover and refrigerate overnight to let the oats absorb the liquid.
3. To serve, add ¾ cup of berries and 1 tbsp. of peanut butter to each Mason jar and enjoy.

Nutrition:
Calories: 515 | Fat: 17 g | Protein: 40 g | Sodium: 99 mg | Fiber: 16 g | Carbohydrates: 56 g | Sugar: 15 g

21. Vanilla Cinnamon-Raisin Bagels

Preparation time: 10 minutes
Cooking time: 25 minutes
Servings: 6
Ingredients:

- ¾ cup all-purpose flour, plus more for dusting
- ¼ cup oat flour
- 2 tsp. baking powder
- 1 tsp. ground cinnamon
- ½ tsp. sea salt
- ⅛ tsp. ground nutmeg
- $^1/_3$ cup raisins
- 1 cup non-fat plain Greek yogurt
- 1 tsp. vanilla extract
- 1 large egg, beaten

Direction:

1. Preheat the oven to 375°F (190°C). Lightly grease a donut pan and set it aside.
2. In a medium bowl, mix the all-purpose flour, oat flour, baking powder, cinnamon, salt, nutmeg, and raisins.

3. Add the yogurt and vanilla and mix with a fork until crumbly and well combined.
4. Lightly dust a work surface with flour. Knead the dough, being careful not to overwork it, about 8 times.
5. Divide the dough into 6 pieces. Roll each piece into a 6 to 7-inch rope. Place each dough rope in the donut pan and pinch the ends together to form a complete circle. Brush the dough with the beaten egg.
6. Bake for 20 to 25 minutes, or until lightly browned. Let the bagels cool completely on a wire rack.
7. Store the bagels in an airtight container in the refrigerator for up to 3 days.

Nutrition
Calories: 115 | Fat: 1 g | Protein: 8 g | Sodium: 130 mg | Fiber: 1 g | Carbohydrates: 18 g | Sugar: 3 g

22. Lemony Chia Muffins with Blueberries

Preparation time: 15 minutes
Cooking time: 22 minutes
Servings: 12
Ingredients:
- 2 cups all-purpose flour
- 2 tbsp. chia seeds
- 1 tbsp. lemon zest, plus ½ tbsp. for garnish
- 1 tsp. baking soda
- 1 tsp. baking powder
- ¼ tsp. sea salt
- 1 cup non-fat plain Greek yogurt
- ½ cup, plus 1 tbsp. maple syrup
- ¼ cup olive oil
- 1 tbsp. 1% milk
- 1 large egg, whisked
- 1 tbsp. freshly squeezed lemon juice
- 1 cup fresh blueberries

Directions:
1. Preheat the oven to 375°F (190°C). Line a 12-cup muffin tin with liners. Lightly spray the liners with nonstick cooking spray.
2. In a large bowl, mix the flour, chia seeds, lemon zest, baking soda, baking powder, and salt. Set aside.
3. In a medium bowl, mix the yogurt, maple syrup, olive oil, milk, egg, and lemon juice.
4. Pour the wet ingredients into the dry ingredients and carefully stir until just mixed. Do not overmix. The batter will be thick. If it is too thick, mix in an additional 1 tbsp. of milk.
5. Add the blueberries and gently fold them into the batter with a rubber spatula. Divide the batter equally into the prepared muffin cups, and garnish with remaining lemon zest.
6. Bake for 20 to 22 minutes, or until baked through. Transfer the muffin tin to a wire rack and let cool for 5 minutes before removing the muffins from the pan and cooling completely.

Nutrition
Calories: 193 | Fat: 6 g | Protein: 5 g | Sodium: 161 mg | Fiber: 2 g | Carbohydrates: 30 g | Sugar: 5 g

23. Egg and Strawberry Protein Pancakes

Preparation time: 15 minutes
Cooking time: 12 minutes
Servings: 3
Ingredients:

- 1 cup all-purpose flour
- 1 tbsp. chia seeds
- ½ tsp. baking powder
- ½ tsp. baking soda
- 1 large egg, beaten
- ¾ cup non-fat plain Greek yogurt
- $^1/_3$ cup 1% milk
- 2 tbsp. maple syrup
- 1 tsp. vanilla extract
- 1 cup diced strawberries
- Non-stick cooking spray

Directions:

1. In a large bowl, mix the flour, chia seeds, baking powder, and baking soda.
2. In another bowl, mix the egg, yogurt, milk, maple syrup, and vanilla. Add the wet ingredients to the dry ingredients and mix well. Add the strawberries and carefully fold them into the batter with a rubber spatula. Let the batter sit for 5 minutes.
3. Lightly spray a large skillet with nonstick cooking spray. Pour ¼ cup of batter into the pan and cook until golden brown, 2 to 3 minutes on each side. Repeat with the remaining batter to make a total of 6 pancakes. Serve immediately

Nutrition
Calories: 306 | Fat: 4 g | Protein: 15 g | Sodium: 273 mg | Fiber: 4 g | Carbohydrates: 52 g | Sugar: 7 g

24. Vanilla Peanut Butter and Chocolate Waffles

Preparation time: 10 minutes
Cooking time: 0 minute
Servings: 4
Ingredients:

- 2 tbsp. unsweetened cocoa powder
- 1½ tbsp. baking powder
- ¼ tsp. sea salt
- 1¼ cups 1% milk
- $^2/_3$ cup non-fat plain Greek yogurt, plus more as desired
- 2 large eggs, whisked
- 1 tsp. vanilla extract
- 2 tbsp. dark chocolate chips
- Non-stick cooking spray

- 4 tbsp. creamy 100% all-natural peanut butter

Direction:

1. Preheat the waffle maker according to the manufacturer's instructions.
2. In a large bowl, mix the flour, cocoa powder, baking powder, and salt.
3. In another bowl, mix the milk, Greek yogurt, eggs, and vanilla. Pour the wet ingredients into the dry ingredients. Add the chocolate chips and carefully stir until just combined. Do not overmix.
4. Lightly spray the hot waffle maker with nonstick cooking spray. Pour ½ cup of batter into the center of the waffle maker and cook according to the manufacturer's instructions. Repeat with the remaining batter. Cut each waffle into 4 sections. Place 6 sections on each plate, spread 1 tbsp. of peanut butter on each serving, and top with extra Greek yogurt, as desired.

Nutrition

Calories: 432 | Fat: 13 g | Protein: 21 g | Sodium: 265 mg | Fiber: 4 g | Carbohydrates: 60 g | Sugar: 5 g

Chapter 5.   Vegetarian diet

25.   Macro Red Curry

Preparation time: 20 minutes
Cooking time: 15–20 minutes
Servings: 6
Ingredients:

- 1 cup broccoli florets
- 1 large handful of fresh spinach
- 4 Tbsp. coconut oil
- 1/4 medium onion
- 1 tsp. garlic, minced
- 1 tsp. fresh ginger, peeled and minced
- 2 tsp. soy sauce
- 1 Tbsp. red curry paste
- 1/2 cup coconut cream

Directions:

1. Add half the coconut oil to a saucepan and heat over medium-high heat.
2. When the oil is hot, put the onion into the pan and sauté for 3–4 minutes, until it is semi-translucent.
3. Sauté garlic, stirring, just until fragrant, about 30 seconds.
4. Lower the heat to medium-low and add broccoli florets. Sauté, stirring, for about 1–2 minutes.
5. Now, add the red curry paste. Sauté until the paste is fragrant, then mix everything.
6. Add the spinach on top of the vegetable mixture. When the spinach begins to wilt, add the coconut cream and stir.
7. Add the rest of the coconut oil, the soy sauce, and the minced ginger. Bring to a simmer for 5–10 minutes.
8. Serve hot.

Nutrition:
Calories: 265 | Fat: 7.1 g | Fiber: 6.9 g | Carbohydrates: 2.1 g | Protein: 4.4 g

26.   Sweet-And-Sour Tempeh

Preparation time: 10 minutes
Cooking time: 25 minutes
Servings: 4
Ingredients:
Tempeh:

- 1 package tempeh
- 3/4 cup vegetable broth
- 2 tbsp. soy sauce
- 2 tbsp. olive oil

Sauce:

- 1 can pineapple juice
- 2 tbsp. brown sugar
- 1/4 cup white vinegar

- 1 tbsp. cornstarch
- 1 red bell pepper
- 1 chopped white onion

Directions:
1. Place a skillet on high heat. Pour in the vegetable broth and tempeh in it.
2. Add the soy sauce to the tempeh. Let it cook until it softens. This usually takes 10 minutes.
3. When it is well cooked, remove the tempeh and keep the liquid. We are going to use it for the sauce.
4. Put the tempeh in another skillet placed on medium heat.
5. Sauté it with olive oil and cook until the tempeh is browned. This should take 3 minutes.
6. Place a pot of the reserved liquid from the cooked tempeh on medium heat.
7. Add the pineapple juice, vinegar, brown sugar, and cornstarch. Stir everything together until it's well combined.
8. Let it simmer for 5 minutes.
9. Add the onion and pepper to the sauce.
10. Stir in until the sauce is thick.
11. Reduce the heat, add the cooked tempeh and pineapple chunks to the sauce. Leave it to simmer together.
12. Remove from heat and serve with any grain food of your choice.

Nutrition:
Calories: 312 | Fat: 10 g | Fiber: 4.1 g | Carbohydrates: 2.1 g | Protein: 5.2 g

27.   Mexican Casserole with Black Beans

Preparation time: 20 minutes
Cooking time: 20 minutes
Servings: 6
Ingredients:
- 2 cups minced garlic cloves
- 2 cups Monterey Jack and cheddar
- 3/4 cup salsa
- 2 1/2 cups chopped red pepper
- 2 tsp. ground cumin
- 2 cans black beans
- 12 corn tortillas
- 2 chopped tomatoes
- 1/2 cup sliced black olives
- 2 cups chopped onion

Directions:
1. Preheat the oven to 350°F.
2. Place a large pot over medium heat.
3. Pour the onion, garlic, pepper, cumin, salsa, and black beans in the pot — Cook the ingredients for 3 minutes, stirring frequently.
4. Arrange the tortillas in the baking dish.
5. Ensure they are well spaced and even overlapping the dish if necessary.
6. Spread half of the bean's mixture on the tortillas. Sprinkle with the cheddar.

7. Repeat the process across the tortillas until everything is well stuffed.
8. Cover the baking dish with foil paper and place it in the oven.
9. Bake it for 15 minutes. Remove from the oven to cool down a bit.
10. Garnish the casserole with olives and tomatoes

Nutrition:
Calories: 325 | Fat: 9.4 g | Fiber: 11.2 g | Carbohydrates: 3.1 g | Protein: 12.6 g

28. Baked Zucchini Gratin

Preparation time: 25 minutes
Cooking time: 30 minutes
Servings: 2
Ingredients:

- 1 large zucchini, cut into 1/4-inch-thick slices
- Pink Himalayan salt
- 1-ounce Brie cheese, rind trimmed off
- 1 tbsp. butter
- Freshly ground black pepper
- 1/3 cup shredded Gruyere cheese
- 1/4 cup crushed pork rinds

Directions:
1. Preheat the oven to 400°F.

2. When the zucchini has been "weeping" for about 30 minutes, in a small saucepan over medium-low heat, heat the Brie and butter, occasionally stirring, until the cheese has melted.
3. The mixture is thoroughly combined for about 2 minutes.
4. Arrange the zucchini in an 8-inch baking dish, so the zucchini slices are overlapping a bit.
5. Season with pepper.
6. Pour the Brie mixture over the zucchini, and top with the shredded Gruyere cheese.
7. Sprinkle the crushed pork rinds over the top.
8. Bake for about 25 minutes, until the dish is bubbling and the top is nicely browned, and serve.

Nutrition:
Calories: 324 | Fat: 11.5 g | Fiber: 5.1 g | Carbohydrates: 2.2 g | Protein: 5.1 g

29.   Veggie Greek Moussaka

Preparation time: 20 minutes
Cooking time: 30 minutes
Servings: 6
Ingredients:

- 2 large eggplants, cut into strips
- 1 cup diced celery
- 1 cup diced carrots
- 1 small white onion, chopped
- 3 eggs
- 1 tsp. olive oil
- 2 cups grated Parmesan
- 1 cup ricotta cheese
- 4 garlic cloves, minced
- 1 tsp. Italian seasoning blend
- Salt to taste

Sauce:

- 1/2 cups heavy cream
- 1/4 cup butter, melted
- 1 cup grated mozzarella cheese
- 2 tsp. Italian seasoning
- 3/4 cup almond flour

Directions:

1. Preheat the oven to 350°F.
2. Lay the eggplant strips, sprinkle with salt, and let sit there to exude liquid. Heat olive oil heat and sauté the onion, celery, garlic, and carrots for 5 minutes.
3. Mix the eggs, 1 cup of Parmesan cheese, ricotta cheese, and salt in a bowl; set aside.
4. Pour the heavy cream into a pot and bring to heat over a medium fire while continually stirring.
5. Stir in the remaining Parmesan cheese and one tsp. of Italian seasoning. Turn the heat off and set it aside.
6. To lay the moussaka, spread a small amount of the sauce at the bottom of the baking dish.
7. Pat dry the eggplant strips and make a single layer on the sauce.
8. A layer of ricotta cheese must be spread on the eggplants, sprinkle some veggies on it, and repeat everything
9. In a small bowl, evenly mix the melted butter, almond flour, and one tsp. of Italian seasoning.
10. Spread the top of the moussaka layers with it and sprinkle the top with mozzarella cheese.
11. Bake for 25 minutes until the cheese is slightly burned. Slice the moussaka and serve warm.

Nutrition:
Calories: 398 | Fat: 15.1 g | Fiber: 11.3 g | Carbohydrates: 3.1 g | Protein: 5.9 g

30.   Gouda Cauliflower Casserole

Preparation time: 15 minutes
Cooking time: 15 minutes
Servings: 4
Ingredients:

- 2 heads cauliflower, cut into florets
- 1/3 cup butter, cubed
- 2 tbsp. melted butter
- 1 white onion, chopped
- Salt and black pepper to taste
- 1/4 almond milk
- 1/2 cup almond flour
- 1 1/2 cups grated gouda cheese

Directions:

1. Preheat the oven to 350°F and put the cauliflower florets in a large microwave-safe bowl.
2. Sprinkle with a bit of water, and steam in the microwave for 4 to 5 minutes.
3. Melt the 1/3 cup of butter in a saucepan over medium heat and sauté the onion for 3 minutes.
4. Add the cauliflower, season with salt and black pepper, and mix in almond milk. Simmer for 3 minutes.
5. Mix the remaining melted butter with almond flour.
6. Stir into the cauliflower as well as half of the cheese. Sprinkle the top with the remaining cheese and bake for 10 minutes until the cheese has melted and golden brown.
7. Plate the bake and serve with salad.

Nutrition:
Calories: 349 | Fat: 9.4 g | Fiber: 12.1 g | Carbohydrates: 4.1 g | Protein: 10 g

31.   Spinach and Zucchini Lasagna

Preparation time: 15 minutes
Cooking time: 30 minutes
Servings: 4
Ingredients:

- 2 zucchinis, sliced
- Salt and black pepper to taste
- 2 cups ricotta cheese
- 2 cups shredded mozzarella cheese
- 3 cups tomato sauce
- 1 cup baby spinach

Directions:

1. Preheat the oven to 375°F and grease a baking dish with cooking spray.

2. Put the zucchini slices in a colander and sprinkle with salt.
3. Let sit and drain liquid for 5 minutes and pat dry with paper towels.
4. Mix the ricotta, mozzarella cheese, salt, and black pepper to evenly combine and spread 1/4 cup of the mixture in the bottom of the baking dish.
5. Layer 1/3 of the zucchini slices on top spread 1 cup of tomato sauce over, and scatter a 1/3 cup of spinach on top. Repeat process.
6. Grease one end of foil with cooking spray and cover the baking dish with the foil.
7. Let it bake for about 35 minutes. And bake further for 5 to 10 minutes or until the cheese has a nice golden-brown color.
8. Remove the dish, sit for 5 minutes, make slices of the lasagna, and serve warm.

Nutrition:
Calories: 376 | Fat: 14.1 g | Fiber: 11.3 g | Carbohydrates: 2.1 g | Protein: 9.5 g

32. Lemon Cauliflower "Couscous" with Halloumi

Preparation time: 5 minutes
Cooking time: 5 minutes
Servings: 2
Ingredients:

- 4 oz. halloumi, sliced
- 1 Cauliflower head, cut into small florets
- 1/4 cup chopped cilantro
- 1/4 cup chopped parsley
- 1/4 cup chopped mint
- 1/2 lemon juiced
- Salt and black pepper to taste
- Sliced avocado to garnish

Directions:
1. Heat the pan and add oil
2. Add the halloumi and fry on both sides until golden brown, set aside. Turn the heat off.
3. Next, pour the cauliflower florets in a food processor and pulse until it crumbles and resembles couscous.
4. Transfer to a bowl and steam in the microwave for 2 minutes.
5. They should be slightly cooked but crunchy.
6. Stir in the cilantro, parsley, mint, lemon juice, salt, and black pepper.
7. Garnish the couscous with avocado slices and serve with grilled halloumi and vegetable sauce.

Nutrition:
Calories: 312 | Fat: 9.4 g | Fiber: 11.9 g | Carbohydrates: 1.2 g | Protein: 8.5 g

33. Spicy Cauliflower Steaks with Steamed Green Beans

Preparation time: 15 minutes
Cooking time: 20 minutes
Servings: 4
Ingredients:

- 2 heads cauliflower, sliced lengthwise into 'steaks.'
- 1/4 cup olive oil
- 1/4 cup chili sauce
- 2 tsp. erythritol
- Salt and black pepper to taste
- 2 shallots, diced
- A bunch green beans, trimmed
- 1 tbsp. fresh lemon juice
- 1 cup water
- 1 Dried parsley to garnish

Directions:

1. In a bowl or container, mix the olive oil, chili sauce, and erythritol.
2. Brush the cauliflower with the mixture. Grill for 6 minutes. Flip the cauliflower, cook further for 6 minutes.
3. Let the water boil, place the green beans in a sieve, and set over the steam from the boiling water.
4. Cover with a clean napkin to keep the steam trapped in the sieve.
5. Cook for 6 minutes.
6. After, remove to a bowl and toss with lemon juice.
7. Remove the grilled caulis to a plate; sprinkle with salt, pepper, shallots, and parsley. Serve with the steamed green beans.

Nutrition:
Calories: 329 | Fat: 10.4 g | Fiber: 3.1 g | Carbohydrates: 4.2 g | Protein: 8.4 g

34. Cheesy Cauliflower Falafel

Preparation time: 20 minutes
Cooking time: 15 minutes
Servings: 4
Ingredients:

- 1 head cauliflower, cut into florets
- 1/3 cup silvered ground almonds
- 1 tbsp. cheddar cheese, shredded
- 1/2 tsp. mixed spice
- Salt and chili pepper to taste
- 1 tbsp. coconut flour
- 2 fresh eggs
- 1 tbsp. ghee

Directions:

1. Blend the florets in a blender until a grain meal consistency is formed.
2. Pour the rice in a bowl, add the ground almonds, mixed spice, salt, cheddar cheese, chili pepper, coconut flour, and mix until evenly combined.

3. Beat the eggs in a bowl until creamy in color and mix with the cauliflower mixture.
4. Shape 1/4 cup each into patties.
5. Melt ghee and fry the patties for 5 minutes on each side to be firm and browned.
6. Remove onto a wire rack to cool, share into serving plates, and top with tahini sauce.

Nutrition:
Calories: 287 | Fat: 9.2 g | Fiber: 4.1 g | Carbohydrates: 3.2 g | Protein: 13.2 g

35. Tofu Sesame Skewers with Warm Kale Salad

Preparation time: 2 hrs.
Cooking time: 25 minutes
Servings: 4
Ingredients:
- 14 oz. Firm tofu
- 4 tsp. sesame oil
- 1 lemon, juiced
- 1 tbsp. sugar-free soy sauce
- 1 tsp. garlic powder
- 1 tbsp. coconut flour
- 1/2 cup sesame seeds

Warm Kale Salad:
- 2 cups chopped kale
- 2 tsp. + 2 tsp. olive oil
- 1 white onion, thinly sliced
- 2 garlic cloves, minced

- 1 cup sliced white mushrooms
- 1 tsp. chopped rosemary
- Salt and black pepper to season
- 1 tbsp. balsamic vinegar

Directions:
1. In a bowl, mix sesame oil, lemon juice, soy sauce, garlic powder, and coconut flour.
2. Wrap the tofu in a paper towel, squeeze out as much liquid from it, and cut it into strips.
3. Stick on the skewers, height-wise.
4. Place onto a plate, pour the soy sauce mixture over, and turn in the sauce to be adequately coated.
5. Heat the griddle pan over high heat.
6. Pour the sesame seeds into a plate and roll the tofu skewers in the seeds for a generous coat.
7. Grill the tofu in the griddle pan to be golden brown on both sides, about 12 minutes.
8. Heat 2 tbsp. of olive oil in a skillet over medium heat and sauté onion to begin browning for 10 minutes with continuous stirring.
9. Add the remaining olive oil and mushrooms.
10. Continue cooking for 10 minutes. Add garlic, rosemary, salt, pepper, and balsamic vinegar.
11. Cook for 1 minute.
12. Put the kale in a salad bowl; when the onion mixture is ready, pour it on the kale and toss well.
13. Serve the tofu skewers with the warm kale salad and a peanut butter dipping sauce.

Nutrition:
Calories: 276 | Fat: 11.9 g | Fiber: 9.4 g | Carbohydrates: 21 g | Protein: 10.3 g

36. Eggplant Pizza with Tofu

Preparation time: 15 minutes
Cooking time: 45 minutes
Servings: 2
Ingredients:

- 2 eggplants, sliced
- 1/3 cup butter, melted
- 2 garlic cloves, minced
- 1 red onion
- 12 oz. tofu, chopped
- 2 Oz. tomato sauce
- Salt and black pepper to taste
- 1/2 tsp. cinnamon powder
- 1 cup Parmesan cheese, shredded
- 1/4 cup dried oregano

Directions:

1. Preheat the oven to 400°F. Lay the eggplant slices on a baking sheet and brush with some butter. Bake in the oven until lightly browned, about 20 minutes.
2. Heat the remaining butter in a skillet; sauté garlic and onion until fragrant and soft, about 3 minutes.

3. Stir in the tofu and cook for 3 minutes. Add the tomato sauce, salt, and black pepper. Simmer for 10 minutes.
4. Sprinkle with Parmesan cheese and oregano. Bake for 10 minutes.

Nutrition:
Calories: 321 | Fat: 11.3 g | Fiber: 8.4 g | Carbohydrates: 4.3 g | Protein: 10.1 g

37. Brussel Sprouts with Spiced Halloumi

Preparation time: 20 minutes
Cooking time: 30 minutes
Servings: 2
Ingredients:

- 10 oz. halloumi cheese, sliced
- 2 tbsp. coconut oil
- 1/2 cup unsweetened coconut, shredded
- 1 tsp. chili powder
- 1/2 tsp. onion powder
- 1/2 pound Brussels sprouts, shredded
- 4 oz. butter
- Salt and black pepper to taste
- 2 Lemon wedges for serving

Directions:

1. In a bowl, mix the shredded coconut, chili powder, salt, coconut oil, and onion powder.

2. Then, toss the halloumi slices in the spice mixture.
3. The grill pan must be heated then cook the coated halloumi cheese for 2–3 minutes.
4. Transfer to a plate to keep warm.
5. The half butter must be melted in a pan, add, and sauté the Brussels sprouts until slightly caramelized.
6. Then, season with salt and black pepper.
7. Dish the Brussels sprouts into serving plates with the halloumi cheese and lemon wedges.
8. Melt left butter and drizzle over the Brussels sprouts and halloumi cheese. Serve.

Nutrition:
Calories: 276 | Fat: 9.5 g | Fiber: 9.1 g | Carbohydrates: 4.1 g | Protein: 5.4 g

38.   Vegetable Patties

Preparation time: 15 minutes
Cooking time: 20 minutes
Servings: 4
Ingredients:
- 2 tbsp. olive oil
- 1 onion, chopped
- 1 garlic clove, minced
- 1/2 head cauliflower, grated
- 1 carrot, shredded
- 1 tbsp. coconut flour
- 1/2 cup Gruyere cheese, shredded
- 1/2 cup Parmesan cheese, grated
- 3 eggs, beaten
- 1/2 tsp. dried rosemary
- Salt and black pepper, to taste

Directions:
1. Cook onion and garlic in warm olive oil over medium heat, until soft, for about 3 minutes.
2. Stir in grated cauliflower and carrot and cook for a minute; allow cooling and set aside.
3. To the cooled vegetables, add the rest of the ingredients, form balls from the mixture, then press each ball to form a burger patty.
4. Set oven to 400 F and bake the burgers for 20 minutes.
5. Flip and bake for another 10 minutes or until the top becomes golden brown.

Nutrition:
Calories: 315 | Fat: 12.1 g | Fiber: 8.6 g | Carbohydrates: 3.3 g | Protein: 5.8 g

39. Vegan Sandwich with Tofu & Lettuce Slaw

Preparation time: 15 minutes
Cooking time: 15 minutes
Servings: 2
Ingredients:

- 1/4-pound firm tofu, sliced
- 2 low carb buns
- 1 tbsp. olive oil

Marinade:

- 2 tbsp. olive oil
- Salt and black pepper to taste
- 1 tsp. allspice
- 1/2 tbsp. xylitol
- 1 tsp. thyme, chopped
- 1 habanero pepper, seeded and minced
- 2 green onions, thinly sliced
- 1 garlic clove

Lettuce slaw:

- 1/2 small iceberg lettuce, shredded
- 1/2 carrot, grated
- 1/2 red onion, grated
- 2 tsp. liquid stevia
- 1 tbsp. lemon juice
- 2 tbsp. olive oil
- 1/2 tsp. Dijon mustard
- Salt and black pepper to taste

Directions:

1. Put the tofu slices in a bowl.
2. Blend the marinade ingredients for a minute.
3. Cover the tofu with this mixture and place it in the fridge to marinate for 1 hour.
4. In a container, combine the lemon juice, stevia, olive oil, Dijon mustard, salt, and pepper.
5. Stir in the lettuce, carrot, and onion; set aside.
6. Heat oil, cook the tofu on both sides for 6 minutes in total.
7. Remove to a plate.
8. In the buns, add the tofu and top with the slaw. Close the buns and serve.

Nutrition:
Calories: 315 | Fat: 10.4 g | Fiber: 15.1 g | Carbohydrates: 9.4 g | Protein: 8.4 g

40. Pizza Bianca

Preparation time: 10 minutes
Cooking time: 10 minutes
Servings: 2
Ingredients:

- 2 tbsp. olive oil
- 4 eggs
- 2 tbsp. water
- 1 jalapeño pepper, diced

- 1/4 cup mozzarella cheese, shredded
- 2 chives, chopped
- 2 cups egg Alfredo sauce
- 1/2 tsp. oregano
- 1/2 cup mushrooms, sliced

Directions:

1. Preheat oven to 360°F.
2. In a bowl, whisk eggs, water, and oregano. Heat the olive oil in a large skillet.
3. The egg mixture must be poured in then let it cook until set, flipping once.
4. Remove and spread the Alfredo sauce and jalapeño pepper all over.
5. Top with mozzarella cheese, mushrooms and chives. Let it bake for 10 minutes

Nutrition:

Calories: 314 | Fat: 15.6 g | Fiber: 10.3 g | Carbohydrates: 5.9 g | Protein: 10.4 g

41.   Pumpkin and Cauliflower Curry

Preparation time: 15 minutes
Cooking time: 7 to 8 hours
Servings: 6
Ingredients:

- 1 tbsp. extra-virgin olive oil
- 4 cups coconut milk
- 1 cup diced pumpkin
- 1 cup cauliflower florets
- 1 red bell pepper, diced
- 1 zucchini, diced
- 1 sweet onion, chopped
- 1 tsp. grated fresh ginger
- 1 tsp. minced garlic
- 1 tbsp. curry powder
- 2 cups shredded spinach
- 1 avocado, **Directions:**

1. Lightly grease the insert of the slow cooker with olive oil.
2. Add the coconut milk, pumpkin, cauliflower, bell pepper, zucchini, onion, ginger, garlic, and curry powder.
3. Cover and cook on low for 7 to 8 hours.
4. Stir in the spinach.
5. Garnish each bowl with a spoonful of avocado and serve.

Nutrition:

Calories: 501 | Fat: 44.0 g | Protein: 7.0 g | Carbs: 19.0 g | Net carbs: 9.0 g | Fiber: 10.0 g

42. Cauliflower Egg Bake

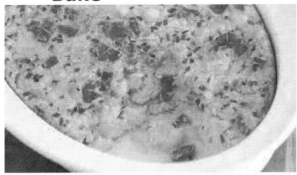

Preparation time: 10 minutes
Cooking time: 25 minutes
Servings: 6
Ingredients:

- 1½ pounds (680 g) cauliflower, broken into small florets
- ½ cup Greek yogurt
- 4 eggs, beaten
- 6 ounces (170 g) ham, diced
- 1 cup Swiss cheese, preferably freshly grated

Directions:

1. Place the cauliflower into a deep saucepan; cover with water and bring to a boil over high heat; immediately reduce the heat to medium-low.
2. Let it simmer, covered, for approximately 6 minutes. Drain and mash with a potato masher.
3. Add in the yogurt, eggs, and ham; stir until everything is well combined and incorporated.
4. Scrape the mixture into a lightly greased casserole dish. Top with the grated Swiss cheese and transfer to a preheated at 390°F (199°C) oven.
5. Bake for 15 to 20 minutes or until cheese bubbles and browns. Bon appétit!

Nutrition:
Calories: 237 | Fat: 13.6 g | Protein: 20.2 g | Carbs: 7.1 g | Net carbs: 4.8 g | Fiber: 2.3 g

43. Zucchini Casserole

Preparation Time: 15 minutes
Cooking time: 45 minutes
Servings: 4
Ingredients:

- Non-stick cooking spray
- 2 cups zucchini, thinly sliced
- 2 tbsp. leeks, sliced
- ½ tsp. salt
- Freshly ground black pepper, to taste
- ½ tsp. dried basil
- ½ tsp. dried oregano
- ½ cup Cheddar cheese, grated
- ¼ cup heavy cream
- 4 tbsp. Parmesan cheese, freshly grated
- 1 tbsp. butter, room temperature
- 1 tsp. fresh garlic, minced

Directions:

1. Start by preheating your oven to 370°F (188°C). Lightly grease a casserole dish with a non-stick cooking spray.
2. Place 1 cup of the zucchini slices in the dish; add 1 tbsp. of leeks;

sprinkle with salt, pepper, basil, and oregano. Top with ¼ cup of Cheddar cheese. Repeat the layers one more time.
3. In a mixing dish, thoroughly whisk the heavy cream with Parmesan, butter, and garlic. Spread this mixture over the zucchini layer and cheese layers.
4. Place in the preheated oven and bake for about 40 to 45 minutes until the edges are nicely browned. Sprinkle with chopped chives, if desired. Bon appétit!

Nutrition:
Calories: 156 | Fat: 12.8 g | Protein: 7.5 g | Carbs: 3.6 g | Net Carbs: 2.8 g | Fiber: 0.8 g

44. Chinese Cauliflower Rice with Eggs

Preparation Time: 7 minutes
Cooking time: 8 minutes
Servings: 3
Ingredients:
- ½ pound (227 g) fresh cauliflower
- 1 tbsp. sesame oil
- ½ cup leeks, chopped
- 1 garlic, pressed
- Sea salt and freshly ground black pepper, to taste
- ½ tsp. Chinese five-spice powder
- 1 tsp. oyster sauce
- ½ tsp. light soy sauce
- 1 tbsp. Shaoxing wine
- 3 eggs

Directions:
1. Pulse the cauliflower in a food processor until it resembles rice.
2. Heat the sesame oil in a pan over medium-high heat; sauté the leeks and garlic for 2 to 3 minutes. Add the prepared cauliflower rice to the pan, along with salt, black pepper, and Chinese five-spice powder.
3. Next, add oyster sauce, soy sauce, and wine. Let it cook, stirring occasionally, until the cauliflower is crisp-tender, about 5 minutes.
4. Then, add the eggs to the pan; stir until everything is well combined. Serve warm and enjoy!

Nutrition:
Calories: 132 | Fat: 8.8 g | Protein: 7.2 g | Carbs: 6.2 g | Net Carbs: 4.4 g | Fiber: 1.8 g

45. Mushroom Stroganoff

Preparation Time: 5 minutes
Cooking time: 10 minutes
Servings: 3
Ingredients:

- 2 tbsp. olive oil
- ½ shallot, diced
- 3 garlic cloves, chopped
- 12 ounces (340 g) brown mushrooms, thinly sliced
- 2 cups tomato sauce

Directions:

1. Heat the olive oil in a stockpot over medium-high heat. Then, sauté the shallot for about 3 minutes until tender and fragrant.
2. Now, stir in the garlic and mushrooms and cook them for 1 minute more until aromatic.
3. Fold in the tomato sauce and bring to a boil; turn the heat to medium-low, cover, and continue to simmer for 5 to 6 minutes.
4. Salt to taste and serve over cauliflower rice if desired. Enjoy!

Nutrition:
Calories: 137 | Fat: 9.3 g | Protein: 3.4 g | Carbs: 7.1 g | Net Carbs: 5.3 g | Fiber: 1.8 g

46. Zucchini Fritters

Preparation Time: 10 minutes
Cooking time: 5 minutes
Servings: 6
Ingredients:

- 1 pound (454 g) zucchini, grated and drained
- 1 egg
- 1 tsp. fresh Italian parsley
- ½ cup almond meal
- ½ cup goat cheese, crumbled
- Sea salt and ground black pepper, to taste
- ½ tsp. red pepper flakes, crushed
- 2 tbsp. olive oil

Directions:

1. Mix all ingredients, except for the olive oil, in a large bowl. Let it sit in your refrigerator for 30 minutes.
2. Heat the oil in a non-stick frying pan over medium heat; scoop the heaped tbsp. of the zucchini mixture into the hot oil.
3. Cook for 3 to 4 minutes; then, gently flip the fritters over and cook on the other side. Cook in a couple of batches.
4. Transfer to a paper towel to soak up any excess grease. Serve and enjoy!

Nutrition:
Calories: 110 | Fat: 8.8 g | Protein: 5.8 g | Carbs: 3.2 g | Net Carbs: 2.2 g | Fiber: 1.0 g

47. Cheese Stuffed Spaghetti Squash

Preparation Time: 15 minutes
Cooking time: 50 to 60 minutes
Servings: 4
Ingredients:

- ½ pound (227 g) spaghetti squash, halved, scoop out seeds
- tsp. olive oil
- ½ cup Mozzarella cheese, shredded
- ½ cup cream cheese
- ½ cup full-fat Greek yogurt
- 2 eggs
- 1 garlic clove, minced
- ½ tsp. cumin
- ½ tsp. basil ½ tsp. mint
- Sea salt and ground black pepper, to taste

Directions:

1. Place the squash halves in a baking pan; drizzle the insides of each squash half with olive oil.
2. Bake in the preheated oven at 370ºF (188°C) for 45 to 50 minutes or until the interiors are easily pierced through with a fork
3. Now, scrape out the spaghetti squash "noodles" from the skin in a mixing bowl. Add the remaining ingredients and mix to combine well.
4. Carefully fill each of the squash halves with the cheese mixture. Bake at 350ºF (180ºC) for 5 to 10 minutes, until the cheese is bubbling and golden brown. Bon appétit!

Nutrition:
Calories: 220 | Fat: 17.6 g | Protein: 9.0 g | Carbs: 6.8 g | Net Carbs: 5.9 g | Fiber: 0.9 g

48. Cottage Kale Stir-Fry

Preparation Time: 10 minutes
Cooking time: 10 minutes
Servings: 3
Ingredients:

- ½ tbsp. olive oil
- 1 tsp. fresh garlic, chopped
- 9 ounces (255 g) kale, torn into pieces
- ½ cup Cottage cheese, creamed
- ½ tsp. sea salt

Directions:

1. Heat the olive oil in a saucepan over a moderate flame. Now, cook the garlic until just tender and aromatic.

2. Then, stir in the kale and continue to cook for about 10 minutes until all liquid evaporates.

3. Fold in the Cottage cheese and salt; stir until everything is heated through. Enjoy!

Nutrition:
Calories: 94 | Fat: 4.5 g | Protein: 7.0 g | Carbs: 6.2 g | Net Carbs: 3.5 g | Fiber: 2.7 g

49. Herbed Eggplant and Kale Bake

Preparation Time: 20 minutes
Cooking time: 40 minutes
Servings: 6
Ingredients:

- 1(¾-pound / 340-g) eggplant, cut into ½-inch slices
- 1 tbsp. olive oil
- 1 tbsp. butter, melted
- 8 ounces (227 g) kale leaves, torn into pieces
- 14 ounces (397 g) garlic-and-tomato pasta sauce, without sugar
- 1/3 cup cream cheese
- 1 cup Asiago cheese, shredded
- ½ cup Gorgonzola cheese, grated
- 2 tbsp. ketchup, without sugar
- 1 tsp. hot pepper
- 1 tsp. basil
- 1 tsp. oregano
- ½ tsp. rosemary

Directions:

1. Place the eggplant slices in a colander and sprinkle them with salt. Allow it to sit for 2 hours. Wipe the eggplant slices with paper towels.

2. Brush the eggplant slices with olive oil; cook in a cast-iron grill pan until nicely browned on both sides, about 5 minutes.

3. Melt the butter in a pan over medium flame. Now, cook the kale leaves until wilted. In a mixing bowl, combine the three types of cheese.

4. Transfer the grilled eggplant slices to a lightly greased baking dish. Top with the kale. Then, add a layer of ½ of cheese blend.

5. Pour the tomato sauce over the cheese layer. Top with the remaining cheese mixture. Sprinkle with seasoning.

6. Bake in the preheated oven at 350°F (180°C) until cheese is bubbling and golden brown, about 35 minutes. Bon appétit!

Nutrition:
Calories: 231 | Fat: 18.6 g | Protein: 10.5 g | Carbs: 6.7 g | Net Carbs: 4.3 g | Fiber: 2.4 g

50. Broccoli and Cauliflower Mash

Preparation Time: 2 minutes
Cooking time: 13 minutes
Servings: 3
Ingredients:
- ½ pound (227 g) broccoli florets
- ½ pound (227 g) cauliflower florets
- Kosher salt and ground black pepper, to season
- ½ tsp. garlic powder
- 1 tsp. shallot powder
- 4 tbsp. whipped cream cheese
- 1½ tbsp. butter

Directions:
1. Microwave the broccoli and cauliflower for about 13 minutes until they have softened completely. Transfer to a food processor and add in the remaining ingredients.
2. Process the ingredients until everything is well combined.
3. Taste and adjust the seasoning. Bon appétit!

Nutrition:
Calories: 163 | Fat: 12.8 g | Protein: 4.7 g | Carbs: 7.2 g | Net Carbs: 3.7 g | Fiber: 3.5 g

51. Cheesy Stuffed Peppers

Preparation Time: 15 minutes
Cooking time: 40 minutes
Servings: 4
Ingredients:
- 2 tbsp. olive oil
- 4 red bell peppers, halved and seeded
- 1 cup ricotta cheese
- ½ cup gorgonzola cheese, crumbled
- 2 garlic cloves, minced
- 1 ½ cups tomatoes, chopped
- 1 tsp. dried basil
- Salt and black pepper, to taste
- ½ tsp. oregano

Directions:
1. Preheat the oven to 350°F.
2. In a bowl, mix garlic, tomatoes, gorgonzola, and ricotta cheeses.
3. Stuff the pepper halves and remove them to the baking dish. Season with oregano, salt, cayenne pepper, black pepper, and basil.
4. Baking Time: 40 minutes

Nutrition:
Calories: 295 | Fat: 12.4 g | Fiber: 10.1 g | Carbs: 5.4 g | Protein: 13.2 g

52.   Creamy Spinach

Preparation Time: 5 minutes
Cooking time: 5 minutes
Servings: 4
Ingredients:

- 1 tbsp. butter, room temperature
- 1 garlic clove, minced
- 10 ounces (283 g) spinach
- ½ tsp. garlic salt
- ¼ tsp. ground black pepper, or more to taste
- ½ tsp. cayenne pepper
- 3 ounces (85 g) cream cheese
- ½ cup double cream

Directions:

1. Melt the butter in a saucepan that is preheated over medium heat. Once hot. Cook garlic for 30 seconds.
2. Now, add the spinach; cover the pan for 2 minutes to let the spinach wilt. Season with salt, black pepper, and cayenne pepper
3. Stir in cheese and cream; stir until the cheese melts. Serve immediately.

Nutrition:
Calories: 167 | Fat: 15.1 g | Protein: 4.4 g | Carbs: 5.0 g | Net Carbs: 3.3 g | Fiber: 1.7 g

53.   Fried Cabbage

Preparation Time: 10 minutes
Cooking time: 15 minutes
Servings: 3
Ingredients:

- 4 ounces (113 g) bacon, diced
- 1 medium-sized onion, chopped
- 2 garlic cloves, minced
- ½ tsp. caraway seeds
- 1 bay laurel
- ½ tsp. cayenne pepper
- 1 pound (454 g) red cabbage, shredded
- ¼ tsp. ground black pepper, to season
- 1 cup beef bone broth

Directions:

1. Heat up a non-stick skillet over a moderate flame. Cook the bacon for 3 to 4 minutes, stirring continuously; set aside.
2. In the same skillet, sauté the onion for 2 to 3 minutes or until it has softened. Now, sauté the garlic and

caraway seeds for 30 seconds more or until aromatic.

3. Then, add in the remaining ingredients and stir to combine. Reduce the temperature to medium-low, cover, and cook for 10 minutes longer; stirring periodically to ensure even cooking.

4. Serve in individual bowls, garnished with the reserved bacon. Enjoy!

Nutrition:
Calories: 242 | Fat: 22.2 g | Protein: 6.5 g | Carbs: 6.8 g | Net Carbs: 4.9 g | Fiber: 1.9 g

Chapter 6. Healthy proteins

54. Chicken Drumsticks in Capocollo

Preparation Time: 10 minutes
Cooking time: 35 minutes
Servings: 5
Ingredients:

- 2 pounds (907 g) chicken drumsticks, skinless and boneless
- 1 garlic clove, peeled and halved
- ½ tsp. smoked paprika
- Coarse sea salt and ground black pepper, to taste
- 10 thin slices capocollo

Directions:

1. Using a sharp kitchen knife, butterfly-cut the chicken drumsticks in half.
2. Lay each chicken drumstick flat on a cutting board and rub garlic halves over the surface of chicken drumsticks. Season with paprika, salt, and black pepper.
3. Lay a slice of capocollo on each piece, pressing lightly. Roll them up and secure them with toothpicks.
4. Bake in the preheated oven at 420ºF (216ºC) for about 15 minutes until the edges of the chicken begin to brown.
5. Turn over and bake for a further 15 to 20 minutes. Bon appétit!

Nutrition:
Calories: 486 | Fat: 33.7 g | Protein: 39.1 g | Carbs: 3.6 g | Net Carbs: 2.6 g | Fiber: 1.0 g

55. Turkey Breast with Tomato-Olive Salsa

Preparation Time: 20 minutes
Cooking time: 10 minutes
Servings: 4
Ingredients:
For turkey:

- 4 boneless turkey. Skinned
- 3 tbsp. olive oil
- Salt
- Pepper

For salsa:

- chopped tomatoes
- ½ diced onions
- 5 ounces pitted and chopped olives
- 2 crushed garlic cloves
- 2 tbsp. chopped basil
- 1 large diced jalapeno
- Pepper

- Salt

Directions:

1. In a bowl, put salt, pepper, and three spoons of oil, mix and coat the turkey with this mixture.

2. Place it on a preheated grill and grill for ten minutes.

3. In another bowl, mix garlic, olives, tomatoes, pepper, and drop the rest of the oil. Sprinkle salt and toss. Serve this salsa with turkey is warm.

Nutrition:
Calories: 387 | Fat: 12.5 g | Fiber: 8.4 g | Carbs: 3.1 g | Protein: 18.6 g

56. Cheddar Bacon Stuffed Chicken Fillets

Preparation Time: 10 minutes
Cooking time: 25 minutes
Servings: 2
Ingredients:

- 2 chicken fillets, skinless and boneless
- ½ tsp. oregano
- ½ tsp. tarragon
- ½ tsp. paprika
- ¼ tsp. ground black pepper
- Sea salt, to taste
- 2 (1-ounce / 28-g) slices bacon
- 2 (1-ounce / 28-g) slices Cheddar cheese
- 1 tomato, sliced

Directions:

1. Sprinkle the chicken fillets with oregano, tarragon, paprika, black pepper, and salt.

2. Place the bacon slices and cheese on each chicken fillet. Roll up the fillets and toothpicks. Place the stuffed chicken fillets on a lightly greased baking pan. Scatter the sliced tomato around the fillets.

3. Bake in the preheated oven at 390°F (199°C) for 15 minutes; turn on the other side and bake an additional 5 to 10 minutes or until the meat is no longer pink.

4. Discard the toothpicks and serve immediately. Bon appétit!

Nutrition:
Calories: 400 | Fat: 23.8 g | Protein: 41.3 g | Carbs: 3.6 g | Net Carbs: 2.4 g | Fiber: 1.2 g

57. Herbed Balsamic Turkey

Preparation Time: 15 minutes
Cooking time: 15 minutes
Servings: 2
Ingredients:

- 1 turkey drumstick, skinless and boneless
- 1 tbsp. balsamic vinegar
- 1 tbsp. whiskey
- 3 tbsp. olive oil
- 1 tbsp. stone ground mustard
- ½ tsp. tarragon
- 1 tsp. rosemary
- 1 tsp. sage
- 1 garlic clove, pressed
- Kosher salt and ground black pepper, to season
- 1 brown onion, peeled and chopped

Directions:
1. Place the turkey drumsticks in a ceramic dish. Toss them with the balsamic vinegar, whiskey, olive oil, mustard, tarragon, rosemary, sage, and garlic.
2. Cover with plastic wrap and refrigerate for 3 hours. Heat your grill to the hottest setting.
3. Grill the turkey drumsticks for about 13 minutes per side. Season with salt and pepper to taste and serve with brown onion. Bon appétit!

Nutrition:
Calories: 389 | Fat: 19.6 g | Protein: 42.0 g | Carbs: 6.0 g | Net Carbs: 4.6 g | Fiber: 1.4 g

58. Chicken and Bell Pepper Kabobs

Preparation Time: 10 minutes
Cooking time: 10 minutes
Servings: 6
Ingredients:
- 2 tbsp. olive oil
- 4 tbsp. dry sherry
- 1 tbsp. stone-ground mustard
- 1½ pounds (680 g) chicken, skinless, boneless, and cubed
- 2 red onions, cut into wedges
- 1 green bell pepper, cut into 1-inch pieces
- 1 red bell pepper, cut into 1-inch pieces
- 1 yellow bell pepper, cut into 1-inch pieces
- ½ tsp. sea salt
- ¼ tsp. ground black pepper, or more to taste

Directions:
1. In a mixing bowl, combine the olive oil, dry sherry, mustard, and chicken until well coated.
2. Alternate skewering the chicken and vegetables until you run out of

ingredients. Season with salt and black pepper.

3. Preheat your grill to medium-high heat.
4. Place the kabobs on the grill, flipping every 2 minutes, and cook to desired doneness. Serve warm.

Nutrition:
Calories: 201 | Fat: 8.2 g | Protein: 24.3 g | Carbs: 7.0 g | Net Carbs: 5.7 g | Fiber: 1.3 g

59. Turkish Chicken Thigh Kebabs

Preparation Time: 15 minutes
Cooking time: 9 to 12 minutes
Servings: 2
Ingredients:

- 1 pound (454 g) chicken thighs, boneless, skinless, and halved
- ½ cup Greek yogurt
- Sea salt, to taste
- 1 tbsp. Aleppo red pepper flakes
- ½ tsp. ground black pepper
- ¼ tsp. dried oregano
- ½ tsp. mustard seeds
- 1/8 tsp. ground cinnamon
- ½ tsp. sumac
- 2 Roma tomatoes, chopped
- 2 tbsp. olive oil
- 1½ ounces (43 g) Swiss cheese, sliced

Directions:

1. Place the chicken thighs, yogurt, salt, red pepper flakes, black pepper, oregano, mustard seeds, cinnamon, sumac, tomatoes, and olive oil in a ceramic dish. Cover and let it marinate in your refrigerator for 4 hours.
2. Preheat your grill for medium-high heat and lightly oil the grate. Thread the chicken thighs onto skewers, making a thick log shape.
3. Cook your kebabs for 3 or 4 minutes; turn over and continue cooking for 3 to 4 minutes more. An instant-read thermometer should read about 165°F (74ºC).
4. Add the cheese and let it cook for a further 3 to 4 minutes or until completely melted. Bon appétit!

Nutrition:
Calories: 500 | Fat: 23.3 g | Protein: 61.0 g | Carbs: 6.2 g | Net Carbs: 4.5 g | Fiber: 1.7 g

60. Chicken Thigh and Kale Stew

Preparation Time: 20 minutes
Cooking time: 6 hours
Servings: 6
Ingredients:

- 3 tbsp. extra-virgin olive oil, divided

- 1 pound (454 g) boneless chicken thighs, diced into 1½-inch pieces
- ½ sweet onion, chopped
- 2 tsp. minced garlic
- 2 cups chicken broth
- 2 celery stalks, diced
- 1 carrot, diced
- 1 tsp. dried thyme
- 1 cup shredded kale
- 1 cup coconut cream
- Salt, for seasoning
- Freshly ground black pepper, for seasoning

Directions:
1. Lightly grease the insert of the slow cooker with 1 tbsp. of the olive oil.
2. In a large skillet over medium-high heat, heat the remaining 2 tbsp. of the olive oil. Add the chicken and sauté until it is just cooked for about 7 minutes.
3. Add the onion and garlic and sauté for an additional 3 minutes.
4. Transfer the chicken mixture to the insert, and stir in the broth, celery, carrot, and thyme.
5. Cover and cook on low for 6 hours.
6. Stir in the kale and coconut cream.
7. Season with salt and pepper, and serve warm.

Nutrition:
Calories: 277 | Fat: 22.0 g | Protein: 17.0 g | Carbs: 6.0 g | Net Carbs: 4.0 g | Fiber: 2.0 g

61.   Turkey Meatballs

Preparation Time: 15 minutes
Cooking time: 20 minutes
Servings: 2
Ingredients:
- 1 pound ground turkey
- 1 tbsp. fish sauce
- 1 diced onion
- 2 tbsp. soy sauce
- ½ almond flour
- 1/8 cup ground beef
- ½ tsp. garlic powder
- ½ tsp. salt
- ½ tsp. ground ginger
- ½ tsp. thyme
- ½ tsp. curry
- 2 tbsp. olive oil

Directions:
1. Combine ground turkey, fish sauce, one diced onion, soy sauce, ground beef, seasonings, oil, and flour in a large mixing bowl. Mix it thoroughly.
2. Form meatballs depending on preferred size.
3. Heat skillet and pour in 3 tbsp. of oil [you may need more depending on the size of meat balls.

4. Cook meatballs until evenly browned on each side. Serve hot.

Nutrition:
Calories: 281| Fat: 11.6 g | Fiber: 6.9 g | Carbs: 4.6 g | Protein: 15.1 g

62. Chicken Schnitzel

Preparation Time: 15 minutes
Cooking time: 15–20 minutes
Servings: 4
Ingredients:
- 1 tbsp. chopped fresh parsley
- 4 garlic cloves, minced
- 1 tbsp. plain vinegar
- 1 tbsp. coconut aminos
- 2 tsp. sugar-free maple syrup
- 2 tsp. chili pepper
- Salt and black pepper to taste
- 2 tbsp. coconut oil
- 1 lb. asparagus, stiff stems removed
- 4 chicken breasts, skin-on and boneless
- 2 cups grated Mexican cheese blend
- 1 tbsp. mixed sesame seeds
- 1 cup almond flour
- 4 eggs, beaten
- 2 tbsp. avocado oil
- 1 tsp. chili flakes for garnish

Directions:
1. In a bowl, whisk the parsley, garlic, vinegar, coconut aminos, maple syrup, chili pepper, salt, and black pepper. Set aside.
2. Heat the coconut oil in a large skillet and stir-fry the asparagus for 8 to 10 minutes or until tender. Remove the asparagus into a large bowl and toss with the vinegar mixture. Set aside for serving.
3. Cover the chicken breasts in plastic wraps and use a meat tenderizer to pound the chicken until flattened to 2-inch thickness gently.
4. On a plate, mix the Mexican cheese blend and sesame seeds. Dredge the chicken pieces in the almond flour, dip in the egg on both sides, and generously coat in the seed mix.
5. Heat the avocado oil. Cook the chicken until golden brown and cooked within.
6. Divide the asparagus onto four serving plates, place a chicken on each, and garnish with the chili flakes. Serve warm.

Nutrition:
Calories: 451| Fat: 18.5 g | Fiber: 12.9 g | Carbs: 5.9 g | Protein: 19.5 g

63.   Chicken Rollatini

Preparation Time: 15 minutes
Cooking time: 30 minutes
Servings: 4
Ingredients:

- 4 (3-ounce) boneless skinless chicken breasts, pounded to about 1/3 inch thick
- 4 ounces ricotta cheese
- 4 slices prosciutto (4 ounces)
- 1 cup fresh spinach
- ½ cup almond flour
- ½ cup grated Parmesan cheese
- 2 eggs, beaten
- ¼ cup good-quality olive oil

Directions:

1. Preheat the oven. Set the oven temperature to 400°F.
2. Prepare the chicken—Pat the chicken breasts dry with paper towels. Spread ¼ of the ricotta in the middle of each breast.
3. Place the prosciutto over the ricotta and ¼ cup of spinach on the prosciutto.
4. Fold the long edges of the chicken breast over the filling, then roll the chicken breast up to enclose the filling.
5. Place the rolls seam-side down on your work surface.
6. Bread the chicken. On a plate, stir together the almond flour and Parmesan and set it next to the beaten eggs.
7. Carefully dip a chicken roll in the egg, then roll it in the almond flour mixture until it is completely covered.
8. Set the rolls seam-side down on your work surface. Repeat with the other rolls.
9. Brown the rolls. In a medium skillet over medium heat, warm the olive oil.
10. Place the rolls seam-side down in the skillet and brown them on all sides, turning them carefully, about 10 minutes in total.
11. Transfer the rolls, seam-side down, to a 9-by-9-inch baking dish—Bake the chicken rolls for 25 minutes, or until they're cooked through.
12. Serve. Place one chicken roll on each of the four plates and serve them immediately.

Nutrition:
Calories: 365 | Fat: 17.1 g | Fiber: 9.4 g | Carbs: 3.2 g | Protein: 1.4 g

64.   Teriyaki Turkey with Peppers

Preparation Time: 15 minutes
Cooking time: 10 minutes
Servings: 3
Ingredients:

- ¾ pound (340 g) lean ground turkey
- 1 brown onion, chopped
- 1 red bell pepper, deveined and chopped
- 1 serrano pepper, deveined and chopped
- 1 tbsp. rice vinegar
- 1 garlic clove, pressed
- 1 tbsp. sesame oil
- ½ tsp. ground cumin
- ½ tsp. hot sauce
- 2 tbsp. peanut butter
- Sea salt and cayenne pepper, to season
- ½ tsp. celery seeds
- ½ tsp. mustard seeds
- 1 rosemary sprig, leaves chopped
- 2 tbsp. fresh Thai basil snipped

Directions:

1. Heat a medium-sized pan over medium-high heat; once hot, brown the ground turkey for 4 to 6 minutes; reserve.
2. Then cook the onion and peppers in the pan drippings for a further 2 to 3 minutes.
3. Add ¼ cup of cold water to another saucepan and heat over medium heat. Now, stir in vinegar, garlic, sesame oil, cumin, hot sauce, peanut butter, salt, cayenne pepper, celery seeds, and mustard seeds.
4. Let it simmer, stirring occasionally until the mixture begins to bubble slightly. Bring the mixture to a boil; then, immediately remove from the heat and add the cooked ground turkey and sautéed onion/pepper mixture.
5. Ladle into serving bowls and garnish with the rosemary and Thai basil. Enjoy!

Nutrition:
Calories: 411 | Fat: 27.2 g | Protein: 36.6 g | Carbs: 6.5 g | Net Carbs: 5.5 g | Fiber: 1.0 g

65. Salmon with Radish and Arugula Salad

Preparation Time: 15 minutes
Cooking time: 10 minutes
Servings: 4
Ingredients:

- 1 pound (454 g) salmon, cut into 4 steaks each
- 1 cup radishes, sliced
- Salt and black pepper to taste
- 8 green olives, pitted and chopped
- 1 cup arugula
- 2 large tomatoes, diced
- 3 tbsp. red wine vinegar
- 2 green onions, sliced
- 3 tbsp. olive oil
- 2 slices zero carb bread, cubed
- ¼ cup parsley, chopped

Directions:

1. In a bowl, mix the radishes, olives, black pepper, arugula, tomatoes, wine vinegar, green onion, olive oil, bread, and parsley.

2. Let sit for the flavors to incorporate. Season the salmon steaks with salt and pepper; grill on both sides for 8 minutes in total. Serve the salmon on a bed of the radish salad.

Nutrition:
Calories: 339 | Fat: 21.6 g | Protein: 28.4 g | Carbs: 5.3 g | Net Carbs: 3.0 g | Fiber: 2.3 g

66. Halibut Tacos with Cabbage Slaw

Preparation Time: 15 minutes
Cooking time: 6 minutes
Servings: 4
Ingredients:

- 1 tbsp. olive oil
- 1 tsp. chili powder
- 4 halibut fillets, skinless, sliced
- 2 low carb tortillas

Slaw:

- 2 tbsp. red cabbage, shredded
- 1 tbsp. lemon juice
- Salt to taste
- ½ tbsp. extra-virgin olive oil
- ½ carrot, shredded
- 1 tbsp. cilantro, chopped

Directions:

1. Combine red cabbage with salt in a bowl; massage cabbage to tenderize. Add in the remaining slaw ingredient, toss to coat, and set aside.
2. Rub the halibut with olive oil, chili powder, and paprika. Heat a grill pan over medium heat.
3. Add halibut and cook until lightly charred and cooked through, about 3 minutes per side.
4. Divide between the tortillas. Combine all slaw ingredients in a bowl. Split the slaw among the tortillas.

Nutrition:
Calories: 386 | Fat: 25.9 g | Protein: 23.7 g | Carbs: 12.6 g | Net Carbs: 6.4 g | Fiber: 6.2 g

67. Coconut Shrimp Stew

Preparation Time: 15 minutes
Cooking time: 15 minutes
Servings: 6
Ingredients:

- 1 cup coconut milk
- 2 tbsp. lime juice
- ¼ cup diced roasted peppers
- 1½ pounds (680 g) shrimp, peeled and deveined
- ¼ cup olive oil
- 1 garlic clove, minced
- 14 ounces (397 g) diced tomatoes
- 2 tbsp. sriracha sauce
- ¼ cup onions, chopped
- ¼ cup cilantro, chopped
- Fresh dill, chopped to garnish
- Salt and black pepper to taste

Directions:

1. Heat the olive oil in a pot over medium heat. Add onions and, cook for 3 minutes, or until translucent.
2. Add the garlic and cook, for another minute, until soft. Add tomatoes, shrimp, and cilantro. Cook until the shrimp becomes opaque, about 3–4 minutes. Stir in sriracha and coconut milk, and cook, for 2 more minutes. Do NOT bring to a boil. Stir in the lime juice, and season with salt and pepper to taste. Spoon the stew in bowls, garnish with fresh dill, and serve warm.

Nutrition:
Calories: 325 | Fat: 20.9 g | Protein: 22.8 g | Carbs: 6.2 g | Net Carbs: 5.1 g | Fiber: 1.1 g

68. Asparagus and Trout Foil Packets

Preparation Time: 15 minutes
Cooking time: 15 minutes
Servings: 4
Ingredients:

- 1 pound (454 g) asparagus spears
- 1 tbsp. garlic purée
- 1 pound (454 g) deboned trout, butterflied
- Salt and black pepper to taste
- 3 tbsp. olive oil
- 2 sprigs rosemary
- 2 sprigs thyme
- 2 tbsp. butter
- ½ medium red onion, sliced
- 2 lemon slices

Directions:

1. Preheat the oven to 400°F (205ºC). Rub the trout with garlic purée, salt, and black pepper.
2. Prepare two aluminum foil squares. Place the fish on each square. Divide the asparagus and onion between the squares, top with a pinch of salt and pepper, a sprig of rosemary and

thyme, and 1 tbsp. of butter. Also, lay the lemon slices on the fish. Wrap and close the fish packets securely, and place them on a baking sheet. Bake in the oven for 15 minutes, and remove once ready.

Nutrition:
Calories: 495 | Fat: 39.2 g | Protein: 26.9 g | Carbs: 7.5 g | Net Carbs: 4.9 g | Fiber: 2.6 g

69. Pistachio Nut Salmon with Shallot Sauce

Preparation Time: 15 minutes
Cooking time: 30 minutes
Servings: 4
Ingredients:

- 4 salmon fillets
- ½ tsp. pepper
- 1 tsp. salt
- ¼ cup mayonnaise
- ½ cup pistachios, chopped

Sauce:

- 1 shallot, chopped
- 2 tsp. lemon zest
- 1 tbsp. olive oil
- A pinch pepper
- 1 cup heavy cream

Directions:

1. Preheat the oven to 375°F (190°C). Brush the salmon with mayonnaise and season with salt and pepper. Coat with pistachios. Place in a lined baking dish, and bake, for 15 minutes.
2. Heat the olive oil in a saucepan, and sauté the shallots, for a few minutes. Stir in the rest of the sauce ingredients. Bring to a boil, and cook until thickened. Serve the salmon topped with the sauce.

Nutrition:
Calories: 564 | Fat: 47.0 g | Protein: 34.0 g | Carbs: 8.1 g | Net Carbs: 6.0 g | Fiber: 2.1 g

70. Spiced Jalapeno Bites with Tomato

Preparation Time: 10 minutes
Cooking time: 0 minutes
Servings: 4
Ingredients:

- 1 cup turkey ham, chopped
- ¼ jalapeño pepper, minced
- ¼ cup mayonnaise
- 1/3 tbsp. Dijon mustard
- 4 tomatoes, sliced
- Salt and black pepper, to taste
- 1 tbsp. parsley, chopped

Directions:

1. In a bowl, mix the turkey ham, jalapeño pepper, mayo, mustard, salt, and pepper.
2. Spread out the tomato slices on four serving plates, then top each plate with a spoonful of turkey ham mixture.
3. Serve garnished with chopped parsley.

Nutrition:
Calories: 250 | Fat: 14.1 g | Fiber: 3.7 g | Carbs: 4.1 g | Protein: 18.9 g

71. Coconut Crab Cakes

Preparation Time: 20 minutes
Cooking time: 25 minutes
Servings: 4
Ingredients:

- 1 tbsp. minced garlic
- 2 pasteurized eggs
- 2 tsp. coconut oil
- 3/4 cup coconut flakes
- 3/4 cup chopped of spinach
- ¼ pound crabmeat
- ¼ cup chopped leek

- ½ cup extra virgin olive oil
- ½ tsp. pepper
- ¼ onion diced
- Salt

Directions:
1. Pour the crabmeat into a bowl, then add in the coconut flakes and mix well.
2. Whisk eggs in a bowl, then mix in leek and spinach.
3. Season the egg mixture with pepper, two pinches of salt, and garlic.
4. Then, pour the eggs into the crab and stir well.
5. Preheat a pan, heat extra virgin olive, and fry the crab evenly from each side until golden brown. Remove from pan and serve hot.

Nutrition:
Calories: 254 | Fat: 9.5 g | Fiber: 5.4 g | Carbs: 4.1 g | Protein: 8.9 g

72.   Tuna Cakes

Preparation Time: 15 minutes
Cooking time: 10 minutes
Servings: 2
Ingredients:
- 1(15-ounce) can water-packed tuna, drained
- ½ celery stalk, chopped
- 2 tbsp. fresh parsley, chopped
- 1 tsp. fresh dill, chopped
- 2 tbsp. walnuts, chopped
- 2 tbsp. mayonnaise
- 1 organic egg, beaten
- 1 tbsp. butter
- 3 cups lettuce

Directions:
1. For burgers: Add all ingredients (except the butter and lettuce) to a bowl and mix until well combined.
2. Make two equal-sized patties from the mixture.
3. Melt some butter and cook the patties for about 2–3 minutes.
4. Carefully flip the side and cook for about 2–3 minutes.
5. Divide the lettuce onto serving plates.
6. Top each plate with one burger and serve.

Nutrition:
Calories: 267 | Fat: 12.5 g | Fiber: 9.4 g | Carbs: 3.8 g | Protein: 11.5 g

73.   Limey Beef Tacos on a Stick

Preparation Time: 15 minutes
Cooking time: 10 minutes
Servings: 4
Ingredients:

- 1 small white onion, chopped
- Juice of 1 lime
- 1 tsp. ground cumin
- 1 tsp. chili powder
- ½ tsp. garlic powder
- ¼ tsp. sea salt
- ¼ tsp. freshly ground black pepper
- 12 ounces (340 g) beef sirloin tips, cut into 1-inch cubes
- Non-stick cooking spray
- 1 red bell pepper, seeded and cut into 1-inch (16 g) pieces
- 1 large white onion, peeled and cut into 8 wedges

Directions:

1. In a food processor, combine the onion, lime juice, cumin, chili powder, garlic powder, salt, and pepper and puree until smooth.
2. Transfer the mixture to a large zip-top plastic bag. Add the sirloin tips, seal, and use your hands to squish around the beef so it's evenly coated in the marinade. Refrigerate for at least 1 hour.
3. Preheat the broiler. Spray the broiler rack with non-stick cooking spray. Remove the beef from the plastic bag and discard the marinade. Thread the beef, pepper, and onion alternately onto 8 to 12 metal skewers.
4. Place the skewers on the broiler rack and broil for 5 minutes. Turn over the skewers and broil for another 4 to 5 minutes, or until the beef is cooked through.

Nutrition:
Calories: 149 | Fat: 4 g | Protein: 19 g | Sodium: 186 mg | Fiber: 2 g | Carbs: 9 g | Sugar: 3 g

74. Butter and Thyme Steak

Preparation Time: 10 minutes
Cooking time: 11 minutes
Servings: 4
Ingredients:

- 2½ tbsp. olive oil, divided
- 4 (4-ounce/113 g) top sirloin steaks, each 1-inch thick
- ½ tsp. freshly ground black pepper, plus more as needed
- ½ tsp. sea salt, plus more as needed
- 1 sprig fresh rosemary
- 1 sprig fresh thyme
- 2 garlic cloves, minced
- 1 tbsp. butter
- 1 pound (454 g) green beans, trimmed

Directions:

1. Heat 1½ tbsp. of olive oil in a large non-stick skillet over medium-high heat. Season the steaks with pepper and salt. Add the rosemary, thyme, and garlic to the skillet. Add the steak and cook until browned, 3 to 4 minutes on each side.

2. Add the butter and continue to cook the steak, basting the steak with the butter constantly, for 1 to 2 minutes. Remove the skillet from the heat.
3. Bring a large pot of water to a boil over high heat. Add the green beans and cook until tender, 4 to 5 minutes.
4. Drain and toss the green beans with the remaining 1 tbsp. of olive oil and season with salt and pepper to taste.

Nutrition:
Calories: 352| Fat: 24 g | Protein: 26 g | Sodium: 323 mg | Fiber: 3 g | Carbs: 8 g | Sugar: 2 g

75. Oregano with Beef and Bean Chili

Preparation Time: 15 minutes
Cooking time: 32 minutes
Servings: 4
Ingredients:

- 1 tbsp. olive oil
- ½ large white onion, chopped
- 3 garlic cloves, minced
- 1 tbsp. tomato paste
- 1 pound (454 g) extra-lean ground beef
- 1½ tbsp. chili powder

- 1 tsp. ground cumin
- 1 tsp. dried oregano
- ½ tsp. paprika
- Sea salt to taste
- Freshly ground black pepper to taste
- 1 (15-ounce/425 g) can kidney beans, drained and rinsed
- 1 (28-ounce/794 g) can crushed tomatoes

Directions:
1. Heat the oil in a large pot over medium heat. Add the onion and cook, stirring frequently, until soft, 4 to 5 minutes. Add the garlic and cook for 1 minute. Add the tomato paste and stir well.
2. Add the beef and cook, breaking it apart using a wooden spoon, until browned and cooked through for 8 to 10 minutes. Drain any excess fat and return the pot to the heat.
3. Add the chili powder, cumin, oregano, and paprika. Season with salt and pepper to taste. Add the kidney beans and crushed tomatoes, stir to combine, and bring the chili to a boil. Cover the pot, reduce the heat to medium-low, and simmer for 20 to 25 minutes. Season with more salt and pepper, if desired. Spoon into bowls and serve.

Nutrition:
Calories: 215 | Fat: 7 g | Protein: 22 g | Sodium: 272 mg | Fiber: 7 g | Carbs: 18 g | Sugar: 2 g

76.   Creamy Butter and Beef Lettuce Wraps

Preparation Time: 15 minutes
Cooking time: 13 minutes
Servings: 4
Ingredients:
- 2 tbsp. creamy 100% all-natural peanut butter
- 2 tbsp. low-sodium soy sauce
- ½ tsp. freshly squeezed lime juice
- 1 tsp. sriracha
- 2 tbsp. water
- 1 tbsp. olive oil
- 2 scallions, green parts only, finely chopped
- 3 garlic cloves, minced
- 1 pound (454 g) extra-lean ground beef
- Sea salt to taste
- Freshly ground black pepper to taste
- 1 cup canned sliced water chestnuts, drained
- ½ cup shredded carrots
- 12 large Butterhead lettuce leaves
- 3 tbsp. chopped peanuts

Directions:

1. In a small bowl, mix the peanut butter, soy sauce, lime juice, sriracha, and water until mostly smooth. Set aside.
2. Heat the olive oil in a large non-stick skillet over medium-high heat. Add the scallions and garlic and sauté for 1 minute. Add the ground beef and cook, breaking it apart using a wooden spoon, until browned and cooked through for 8 to 10 minutes. Add salt and pepper to taste.
3. Add the peanut butter sauce, water chestnuts, and carrots and cook, stirring frequently, for 1 to 2 minutes.
4. Spoon the mixture into the lettuce leaves and garnish with the peanuts. Serve immediately.

Nutrition:
Calories: 326 | Fat: 18 g | Protein: 31 g | Sodium: 451 mg | Fiber: 3 g | Carbs: 12 g | Sugar: 3 g

77.   Quinoa, Pineapple, and Beef Bowl

Preparation Time: 10 minutes
Cooking time: 16 minutes
Servings: 4

Ingredients:
- 1½ cups quinoa
- 1½ tbsp. olive oil, divided
- 1 pound (454 g) extra-lean ground beef
- ½ tsp. sea salt, plus more as needed
- ¼ tsp. freshly ground black pepper, plus more as needed
- 2 green bell peppers, seeded and chopped
- 2 cups pineapple chunks
- 6 scallions, green parts only, thinly sliced
- $^1/_3$ cup crushed unsalted cashews

Directions:

1. Cook the quinoa according to the package instructions.
2. Heat 1 tbsp. of olive oil in a large non-stick skillet over medium-high heat. Add the ground beef, breaking it apart using a wooden spoon, and cook until browned and cooked through for 8 to 10 minutes. Add the salt and pepper and stir. Transfer to a plate and set aside.
3. In the same skillet, heat the remaining ½ tbsp. of olive oil. Add the bell peppers and sauté until tender, 4 to 6 minutes. Add the pineapple chunks and cook, stirring, for 1 minute.
4. Add the ground beef, scallions, and cashews to the skillet and cook, stirring, until blended, 1 to 2 minutes. Add salt and pepper to taste.
5. Divide the quinoa between 4 bowls. Top with the ground beef mixture and serve immediately.

Nutrition:
Calories: 553 | Fat: 20 g | Protein: 37 g | Sodium: 319 mg | Fiber: 8 g | Carbs: 60 g | Sugar: 7 g

78. Garlicky Cheese and Beef Spaghetti

Preparation Time: 15 minutes
Cooking time: 15 minutes
Servings: 4
Ingredients:

- 8 ounces (227 g) whole-grain spaghetti
- 1 tbsp. olive oil, divided
- 1 pound (454 g) extra-lean ground beef
- Sea salt to taste
- Freshly ground black pepper to taste
- 1 shallot, minced
- 3 garlic cloves, minced
- 1 cup sliced mushrooms
- 1½ cups crushed tomatoes
- ½ cup skim milk
- 2 tsp. balsamic vinegar
- 1 tbsp. Italian seasoning
- ¼ cup grated reduced-fat Parmesan cheese

Directions:

1. Cook the spaghetti according to the package instructions.
2. Heat ½ tbsp. of olive oil in a large non-stick skillet over medium-high heat. Add the ground beef, breaking it apart using a wooden spoon, and cook until browned and cooked through for 8 to 10 minutes. Drain any excess oil. Add salt and pepper and stir. Transfer to a plate and set aside.
3. In the same pan, heat the remaining ½ tbsp. of olive oil over medium-high heat. Add the shallot and sauté until soft, 1 to 2 minutes. Add the garlic and sauté for 1 minute. Add the mushrooms and sauté until soft, 2 to 3 minutes.
4. Add the crushed tomatoes, milk, balsamic vinegar, and Italian seasoning and mix well. Reduce the heat to low and cook until the sauce begins to thicken. Remove from the heat, add the ground beef, and mix well. Add salt and pepper to taste.
5. Divide the pasta between 4 bowls. Top with the beef mixture and top with the Parmesan cheese. Serve hot.

Nutrition:
Calories: 429 | Fat: 11 g | Protein: 36 g | Sodium: 202 mg | Fiber: 7 g | Carbs: 49 g | Sugar: 1 g

79. Spinach and Spicy Mustard Pork Chops

Preparation Time: 15 minutes
Cooking time: 14 minutes
Servings: 4
Ingredients:

- ¼ cup Dijon mustard
- 1½ tbsp. honey
- 1 tsp. freshly squeezed lemon juice
- ¼ tsp. cayenne pepper
- ¼ tsp. freshly ground black pepper
- ¼ tsp. sea salt
- 4 (4-ounce/113 g) pork chops, 1 inch thick
- 2½ tbsp. olive oil, divided
- 2 garlic cloves, minced
- 3 cups sliced white button mushrooms
- 4 cups fresh baby spinach

Directions:

1. Combine the mustard, honey, lemon juice, cayenne pepper, black pepper, and salt in a large zip-top plastic bag. Add the pork, remove as much air as possible, and seal. Carefully shake the bag a few times to coat the pork evenly with the marinade. Refrigerate for at least 1 hour.
2. Remove the pork chops from the plastic bag and discard the marinade. Heat 2 tbsp. of olive oil in a large non-stick skillet over medium heat. Add the pork chops and cook until they reach an internal temperature of 145°F (63°C), 4 to 6 minutes per side. Transfer the chops to a clean cutting board and let rest for 5 minutes before cutting them into slices.
3. In the same skillet, heat the remaining ½ tbsp. of olive oil. Add the garlic and sauté for 1 minute. Add the mushrooms and cook until soft, 2 to 3 minutes. Add the spinach and cook until it wilts for about 1 minute.
4. Divide the spinach between 4 plates and top with the pork chops.

Nutrition:
Calories: 305 | Fat: 17 g | Protein: 28 g | Sodium: 370 mg | Fiber: 2 g | Carbs: 11 g | Sugar: 3 g

80. Garlicky Carrot Pork Fried Rice

Preparation Time: 10 minutes
Cooking time: 15 minutes
Servings: 4
Ingredients:

- 1 cup quick brown rice
- 1½ tbsp. olive oil

- 1 pound (454 g) extra-lean ground pork
- 2 garlic cloves, minced
- 1 cup thinly sliced white button mushrooms
- 1 cup matchstick carrots
- Sea salt to taste
- Freshly ground black pepper to taste
- 2 tbsp. low-sodium soy sauce
- 4 scallions, green parts only, thinly sliced

Directions:
1. Cook the rice according to the package instructions.
2. Heat a large non-stick skillet over medium-high heat until a drop of water sizzles on contact. Add 1 tbsp. of olive oil and use a small basting brush to coat the pan evenly. Add the ground pork, breaking it apart using a wooden spoon, and cook until browned and cooked through for 6 to 8 minutes. Transfer to a plate and set aside. Wipe out the skillet with paper towels and return it to the stovetop.
3. Heat the remaining ½ tbsp. of olive oil in the skillet over medium heat. Add the garlic and sauté for 1 minute. Add the mushrooms and carrots and cook, stirring occasionally, until the mushrooms are soft, 3 to 5 minutes. Season with salt and pepper to taste.
4. Return the pork to the skillet, add the rice and soy sauce, and cook, stirring constantly, until heated through, 1 to 2 minutes.
5. Divide the mixture between 4 bowls, garnish with the scallions, and serve.

Nutrition:
Calories: 380 | Fat: 11 g | Protein: 29 g | Sodium: 356 mg | Fiber: 3 g | Carbs: 42 g | Sugar: 3 g

81.   Milky Sauce Pork

Preparation Time: 15 minutes
Cooking time: 50 minutes
Servings: 6
Ingredients:
- Non-stick cooking spray
- 2 pounds(907 g) extra-lean ground pork
- 1 large egg, beaten
- 1 small white onion, chopped
- ½ cup skim milk
- 1 cup bread crumbs
- ½ tsp. sea salt
- ¼ tsp. freshly ground black pepper
- $^1/_3$ cup barbecue sauce

Directions:
1. Preheat the oven to 350°F (185°C). Lightly spray a baking dish with non-stick cooking spray.

2. In a large bowl, mix the ground pork, egg, onion, milk, bread crumbs, salt, and pepper.
3. Put the pork mixture into the baking dish.
4. Pour the barbecue sauce over the meatloaf, cover with aluminum foil, and bake for 50 to 60 minutes, or until cooked through.

Nutrition:
Calories: 287 | Fat: 8 g | Protein: 36 g | Sodium: 540 mg | Fiber: 1 g | Carbs: 19 g | Sugar: 8 g

Chapter 8.   Desserts

82.   Vanilla Chia Pudding

Preparation Time: 15 Minutes
Cooking time: 7–11 hours
Servings: 5
Ingredients:

- ½ cup strawberries
- 2 cups water
- Sweetener
- ½ cup heavy cream
- Vanilla extract
- ½ cup chia seeds
- 2 tbsp. MCT oil

Directions:

1. Add chia seeds, heavy cream, water, MCT oil, vanilla extract, and sweetener in a bowl. Mix them together. Allow sitting for 7–11 hours. After 11 hours add strawberries. Your dish is ready.

Nutrition:
Calories: 286 | Fat: 7.9 g | Fiber: 5.4 g | Carbs: 2 g | Protein: 34 g

83.   Almond Lemon Blueberry Muffins

Preparation Time: 17 minutes
Cooking time: 2–3 hours
Servings: 3
Ingredients:

- 1 cup almond flour
- 1 large egg
- 3 drops Stevia
- ¼ cup fresh blueberries
- ¼ tsp. lemon zest, grated
- ¼ tsp. pure lemon extract
- ½ cup heavy whipping cream
- 2 tbsp. butter, melted
- ½ tsp. baking powder

Directions:

1. Add egg into a bowl. Whisk well
2. Combine the rest of the ingredients. Whisk well.
3. Pour batter into lined or greased muffin molds. Pour up to 3/4 of the cup.
4. Pour 6 ounces of water into the slow cooker. Place the muffin molds inside the cooker.

5. Close the lid. Set cooker on 'High' option and timer for 2–3 hours.
6. Let it cool in the cooker for a while.
7. Remove from the cooker. Loosen the edges of the muffins. Invert on to a plate and serve.

Nutrition:
Calories: 223 | Fat: 21 g | Carbs: 5 g | Protein: 6 g

84. Choco Lava Cake

Preparation Time: 15 Minutes
Cooking time: 45 minutes
Servings: 4
Ingredients:
- 2 ounces dark chocolate
- 1 tbsp. almond flour
- ¼ cup coconut oil
- ¼ tsp. Vanilla extract
- 2 eggs
- 2 tbsp. Cocoa powder for garnish
- 2 tbsp. sweetener

Directions:
1. Preheat the oven to 190°C. Grease two molds with coconut oil and sprinkle them with cocoa powder. Melt chocolate, coconut oil, and add vanilla to it. Beat eggs and

sweeteners together in a different bowl.
2. Slowly add the chocolate mixture with egg mixture and beat until well mixed. Add the almond flour and mix until incorporated. Fill the molds evenly with the mixture. Bake for 10 minutes. Serve immediately.

Nutrition:
Calories: 126 | Fat: 9 g | Fiber: 5.46 g | Carbs: 2 g | Protein: 114 g

85. Coconut Cup Cakes

Preparation Time: 15 Minutes
Cooking time: 45 minutes
Servings: 4
Ingredients:
Cupcakes:
- 6 tbsp. coconut flour
- ½ cup hot water
- ½ cup unsalted coconut butter
- 1 tsp. vanilla extract
- 1 tbsp. flaxseed
- 1 tsp. baking powder
- 4 tbsp. stevia
- A pinch salt

For icing:
- 1 cup raw cashews
- 2 tbsp. Swerve
- ½ cup whole coconut milk
- 1 tsp. vanilla extract

Directions:
Cupcakes:
1. Preheat the oven to 170°C. Grease 6 cupcake molds. Pour the water over the coconut butter and mix well, then add flaxseed, vanilla, stevia, and salt. Leave the flaxseed for few minutes to stow everything. In another bowl, mix baking powder and coconut flour.
2. Add flour mixture and flaxseed mixture slowly and stir until no lumps are left and everything is smooth. Spread them in molds and bake for 20 to 25 minutes until the top is solid and the edges turn golden. Take them out of the oven and wait a few minutes for them to cool

Icing:
3. Put all ingredients in a blender and blend for about 2–3 minutes until smooth. Add them to cupcakes. Sprinkle with dried coconut if you want

Nutrition:
Calories: 321 | Fat: 15 g | Fiber: 5 g | Carbs: 3 g | Protein: 11 g

86. Easy Chocolate Cheesecake

Preparation Time: 15 Minutes
Cooking time: 1 hour
Servings: 4
Ingredients:
Cheesecake:
- 2½ tbsp. sour cream
- 3 tbsp. Erythritol powder
- 5 tbsp. cream cheese
- 3 tbsp. cocoa powder
- 2 tbsp. butter
- ½ tsp. vanilla extract

Crust:
- 2 tbsp. Almond flour
- Pinch kosher salt
- 2 tsp. cocoa powder
- 2 tsp. butter
- 2 tsp. powdered Erythritol

Directions:
Crust:
1. Roast almond flour in a pan over medium heat until golden for 3 minutes.

2. Pour the roasted almond flour into a small bowl and mix cocoa, sweetener, and salt.
3. Add the butter and mix well.
4. Press into a pastry mold or a plate and refrigerate while the cheesecake is being prepared.

Cake:

1. Put the sour cream in a medium bowl and beat with an electric mixer for 3 minutes.
2. Add cream cheese, butter and beat with an electric mixer until the cream is completely mixed.
3. Add vanilla extract, sweetener, cocoa, and beat until everything is mixed together.
4. Pour the mixture into the mold. Freeze for 20 to 30 minutes.

Nutrition:
Calories: 200 | Fat: 15 g | Fiber: 5 g | Carbs: 2 g | Protein: 11 g

87. Chocolate Chip Brownie

Preparation Time: 15 Minutes
Cooking time: 1 hour
Servings: 4
Ingredients:
- ½ cup MCT oil
- 2 tsp. erythritol
- ½ cup water
- ¼ tsp. baking powder
- 1 tsp. Vanilla extract
- ¼ tsp. salt
- ½ cup coconut flour
- Keto Chocolate chips
- 2 tbsp. cocoa powder

Directions:
1. Mix 1 tbsp. of cocoa powder and 1 tbsp. of MCT oil, mix well. Add a few drops of Vanilla extract, sweetener, and mix them well.
2. Preheat the oven to 180°C. Put MCT oil, water, vanilla extract, coconut flour, chocolate chips, salt, baking powder, and sweetener in a bowl and mix them all well. Let it cool for at least 10 minutes before baking.
3. Cover pan with parchment paper. Stir all mixture in the pan. Bake for 15 minutes. Allow the brownies to cool for 10 minutes before slicing and serving.

Nutrition:
Calories: 213 | Fat: 12 g | Fiber: 3.5 g | Carbs: 3 g | Protein: 21 g

88. Coconut Cookies

Preparation Time: 15 Minutes
Cooking time: 1 hour
Servings: 20
Ingredients:

- 3 cups unsweetened coconut flakes
- ½ cup sugar-free maple syrup
- 1 cup coconut oil

Directions:

1. Layout a large plate or baking tray with parchment paper and set aside. In a large bowl mix all ingredients and mix well.
2. Lightly moisten the hands, then form small balls with the dough and place them on a baking tray at a distance of 1 to 2 inches.
3. Tap on each biscuit with a fork.
4. Cool until firm.

Nutrition:
Calories: 44 | Fat: 14 g | Fiber: 3.5 g | Carbs: 0.5 g | Protein: 11 g

89. Choco Pie

Preparation Time: 15 Minutes
Cooking time: 1 hour
Servings: 6
Ingredients:

- ½ cup dark chocolate
- 2 tsp. stevia powder
- 2 cups coconut milk cream
- 1 tbsp. coconut water
- 1½ cups crushed roasted hazelnuts
- A pinch salt
- 1 tsp. vanilla extract
- 2½ tbsp. water
- 3 tbsp. coconut oil
- 1 tbsp. flaxseed
- 1 tsp. stevia powder
- 1 ½ cups almond flour

Directions:

1. Preheat the oven to 175°C. Cover the baking pan with a parchment sheet. Stir the dry ingredients together in a bowl and mix them well.
2. Combine the flax seeds and water in another small bowl and set aside. Let the seeds get thick.

3. Pour the flax mixture and the melted coconut oil over the dry ingredients and mix well. Firmly press the dough into the mold base.

4. Use a fork to prick the crust. Bake the crust for about 15 minutes until it's firm and slightly browned. Set aside to let it cool.

5. Put roasted hazelnuts in a blender, blend until oil is released and liquid state is obtained.

6. Add melted chocolate and salt. Blend. Put the coconut cream in another bowl. Add vanilla, 1 tbsp. of Coconut water, and sweetener.

7. Beat the cream with the hand blender for 60 seconds or more until it gets soft and fluffy.

8. Carefully stir the cream with the chocolate mixture.

9. Taste it and add some sweetener if needed.

10. Pour the filling over the crust. Freeze for 2 hours until the mixture is ready.

Nutrition:
Calories: 126| Fat: 11 g | Fiber: 3 g | Carbs: 3 g | Protein: 9 g

Chapter 9.   30-Day Meal Plan

Days	Breakfast	Lunch	Dinner	Dessert
1	Almond with Yogurt Parfait	Macro Red Curry	Chicken Drumsticks in Capocollo	Vanilla Chia Pudding
2	Blueberry Fat Bombs	Sweet-And-Sour Tempeh	Turkey Breast with Tomato-Olive Salsa	Choco Lava Cake
3	Cheesy Zucchini Triangles with Garlic Mayo Dip	Mexican Casserole with Black Beans	Cheddar Bacon Stuffed Chicken Fillets	Coconut Cup Cakes
4	Herbed Cheese Chips	Baked Zucchini Gratin	Herbed Balsamic Turkey	Easy Chocolate Cheesecake
5	Cauliflower Poppers	Veggie Greek Moussaka	Chicken and Bell Pepper Kabobs	Chocolate Chip Brownie
6	Crispy Parmesan Chips	Gouda Cauliflower Casserole	Turkish Chicken Thigh Kebabs	Coconut Cookies
7	Tex-Mex Queso Dip	Spinach and Zucchini Lasagna	Chicken Thigh and Kale Stew	Vanilla Chia Pudding
8	Sweet Onion Dip	Lemon Cauliflower "Couscous" with Halloumi	Turkey Meatballs	Choco Lava Cake
9	Keto Trail Mix	Spicy Cauliflower Steaks with Steamed Green Beans	Chicken Schnitzel	Coconut Cup Cakes
10	Cold Cuts and Cheese Pinwheels	Cheesy Cauliflower Falafel	Chicken Rollatini	Easy Chocolate Cheesecake
11	Zucchini Balls with Capers and Bacon	Tofu Sesame Skewers with Warm Kale Salad	Teriyaki Turkey with Peppers	Chocolate Chip Brownie

12	Strawberry Fat Bombs	Eggplant Pizza with Tofu	Salmon with Radish and Arugula Salad	Coconut Cookies
13	Cinnamon Applesauce Oatmeal	Brussel Sprouts with Spiced Halloumi	Halibut Tacos with Cabbage Slaw	Vanilla Chia Pudding
14	Egg and Chocolate French Toast	Vegetable Patties	Coconut Shrimp Stew	Choco Lava Cake
15	Egg and Applesauce Banana Muffins	Vegan Sandwich with Tofu & Lettuce Slaw	Asparagus and Trout Foil Packets	Coconut Cup Cakes
16	Vanilla Whipped Protein Bowl	Pizza Bianca	Pistachio Nut Salmon with Shallot Sauce	Easy Chocolate Cheesecake
17	Egg and Tortilla Spinach Wrap	Pumpkin and Cauliflower Curry	Spiced Jalapeno Bites with Tomato	Chocolate Chip Brownie
18	Banana Shake with Peanut Butter	Cauliflower Egg Bake	Coconut Crab Cakes	Coconut Cookies
19	Spinach with Milk Banana Smoothie	Zucchini Casserole	Tuna Cakes	Vanilla Chia Pudding
20	Raspberry Cheer Overnight Oats	Chinese Cauliflower Rice with Eggs	Chicken Drumsticks in Capocollo	Choco Lava Cake
21	Vanilla Cinnamon-Raisin Bagels	Mushroom Stroganoff	Turkey Breast with Tomato-Olive Salsa	Coconut Cup Cakes
22	Lemony Chia Muffins with Blueberries	Zucchini Fritters	Cheddar Bacon Stuffed Chicken Fillets	Easy Chocolate Cheesecake
23	Egg and Strawberry Protein Pancakes	Cheese Stuffed Spaghetti Squash	Herbed Balsamic Turkey	Chocolate Chip Brownie

24	Vanilla Peanut Butter and Chocolate Waffles	Cottage Kale Stir-Fry	Chicken and Bell Pepper Kabobs	Coconut Cookies
25	Almond with Yogurt Parfait	Herbed Eggplant and Kale Bake	Turkish Chicken Thigh Kebabs	Vanilla Chia Pudding
26	Blueberry Fat Bombs	Broccoli and Cauliflower Mash	Chicken Thigh and Kale Stew	Choco Lava Cake
27	Cheesy Zucchini Triangles with Garlic Mayo Dip	Cheesy Stuffed Peppers	Turkey Meatballs	Coconut Cup Cakes
29	Herbed Cheese Chips	Creamy Spinach	Chicken Schnitzel	Easy Chocolate Cheesecake
30	Cauliflower Poppers	Fried Cabbage	Chicken Rollatini	Chocolate Chip Brownie

Conclusion

The macro diet is a type of weight loss program based on the idea that you must eat in a certain way to be able to lose weight. There are many different types of diets on the market today, but they all share similar methods: you are supposed to count carbohydrates, proteins, and fats within your daily caloric intake for weight loss success.

Some diets recommend counting your grams of carbohydrates, but others count them by how many they make up of your total daily caloric intake.

The macro diet is a different story. Unlike other diets, the macro diet suggests that you only need to count fats within the daily calorie intake to lose weight. Fats are considered essential nutrients, meaning you need them for proper health, yet they can be dangerous if consumed in excess.

For instance, if you are following a weight loss macro diet, you should be eating low-fat foods and food items in order to cut back on the fat calories within your daily caloric intake. The goal is to boost your metabolism as well as burn extra fat off of your body.

Doing this will help in the long run, especially since the weight loss plan requires plenty of exercise and muscle strengthening exercises. This will help increase your metabolism and help you burn extra fat from your body during the course of a day.

The macro diet is extremely popular among persons who are obese or who want to maintain their current weight merely. The reason why the macro diet is so popular is that it offers a perfect balance of healthy foods that will strengthen your body and aid in proper weight loss. Another reason the macro diet has been so well received by many people is that it's a healthy eating plan that can be followed for long periods of time without any problems.

If you want to lose weight, enhance your physical health, or even alleviate the symptoms of any of the following diseases: heart disease, diabetes, cancer, and so on, a macro diet may be the ideal option.

You'll need to know your current weight and body fat percentage before you can calculate your macros. A digital scale, a gym, or a doctor's office can be used to calculate body fat percentage. Lean body mass is calculated by subtracting weight from body fat. The next step is to figure out how many calories your body uses on a daily basis. To lose fat, you'll eat fewer calories than your maintenance level, and to grow muscle, you'll consume more calories. After you've determined your calorie intake, the next step is to track your calorie consumption for the next seven to 10 days. Weigh yourself on day one and day ten to see how you compare.

You've discovered a calorie deficit when you lose weight. This is ideal if you want to lose weight. However, if you lose more than two and a half pounds in a week, you're undereating. You'll want to up the ante on the cuisine.

If you've gained weight, you're consuming more than you should be. Reduce your calorie consumption by a few hundred and try again. Start with a 10–15 percent reduction in calories, eat that amount for a few days, then check your weight again, and so on until you reach your maintenance level.

If your weight remained constant, you have discovered your maintenance intake. Take roughly 200–500 calories out of your overall carbs and fats to lose weight. If you want to gain muscle, increase your caloric intake by 300 calories, with some of those calories going to protein.

Made in the USA
Columbia, SC
03 October 2021